The Alien and Sedition Acts

MODERN LIBRARY FOUNDING DOCUMENTS

The Declaration of Independence and the Constitution of the United States,
with an introduction by Jon Meacham

The Federalist Papers,
with an introduction by Jon Meacham

The Alien and Sedition Acts

With an introduction by
Qian Julie Wang

THE MODERN LIBRARY
NEW YORK

The Modern Library
An imprint of Random House
A division of Penguin Random House LLC
1745 Broadway, New York, NY 10019
modernlibrary.com
randomhousebooks.com
penguinrandomhouse.com

2025 Modern Library Edition

Transcriptions of the Alien and Sedition Acts are reproduced from the official records of the U.S. National Archives and Records Administration and the Library of Congress. Transcriptions of the Kentucky Resolutions, the Virginia Resolutions, Answers of the Several State Legislatures, and Madison's Report on the Virginia Resolutions, as collected in Elliot, Jonathan, ed., *The Debates in the Several State Conventions on the Adoption of the Federal Constitution*, vol. 4 (Washington, DC: 1836), reproduced from the Law Library of Congress.

Hardcover ISBN 979-8-217-15522-4
Ebook ISBN 979-8-217-15523-1

Printed in Canada on acid-free paper

1 2 3 4 5 6 7 8 9

FIRST EDITION

BOOK TEAM: Production editor: Evan Camfield • Managing editor: Rebecca Berlant • Production manager: Maggie Hart • Copy editor: Mimi Lipson • Proofreaders: Christopher Ross, Barbara Jatkola

The authorized representative in the EU for product safety and compliance is Penguin Random House Ireland, Morrison Chambers, 32 Nassau Street, Dublin D02 YH68, Ireland. https://eu-contact.penguin.ie

Contents

Introduction

By Qian Julie Wang

I. Opening

If the Constitution and the Bill of Rights are the shining pillars built of the brightest hopes of our great American project, the Alien and Sedition Acts of 1798 form the dank, dark cellar that houses all the fears, anxieties, and prejudices that have weighed our nation down since its inception. The acts wasted no time in testing our ten-year-old Constitution, placing upon it the weight of a polarized young nation grappling for power and peace.

The acts comprised four separate laws: the Naturalization Act, the Alien Act, the Sedition Act, and the Alien Enemies Act. Although the first three were either quickly repealed or allowed to expire, the fourth remains alive and well to this day. Indeed, the Alien Enemies Act continues to birth some of the darkest chapters in our nation's history, from the internment of Japanese Americans during World War II to the Trump administration's present-day detention and deportation of scores of individuals based on ethnicity and political beliefs.

It is easy to read the story of the Alien and Sedition Acts

and fall into despair, for in so many ways the acts—the sentiment that birthed them and the ways they have been used since—stand against the foundational American principles of due process, free speech, and checks and balances. But that story also speaks to our power and agency, as a people, to resist, and to bend the long arc of history toward justice. We cannot forget that the book of America is still being written. And we become the scribes by virtue of our unrelenting belief in America and her ability to live up to our grandest ideals. Ultimately, the story of the Alien and Sedition Acts is a call to arms for each of us: to stand guard at the gates of justice; to speak truth in the face of attempts to stamp out dissent; and, above all, to protect the most vulnerable among us, for their safety is the bedrock upon which democracy rests.

II. Origins

In 1797, the young nation of America faced a still new but soon to be recurring set of problems—internal division and discord, anxieties about the growing number of immigrants, and fears about war and the import of "foreign values." The preceding decade saw tumult across Europe and as a result, a wave of immigrants—some eighty thousand from the British Isles, sixty thousand of them from Ireland, with many more to follow during the Irish Rebellion of 1798. France was embroiled in revolution, which reached its colonies: in 1791, what was then Saint-Domingue saw the only known historical instance of a slave uprising that led to the creation of an independent nation of former slaves—Haiti. Displaced by the chaos, many French and Haitian immigrants moved to the United States and settled in Philadelphia, forming a sizeable population within what was then the nation's capital.

Buoyed by the promises in the recently ratified Constitution and Bill of Rights, new and established Americans alike largely embraced revolutionary sentiment, seeing uprisings as a sign that similar rights and freedoms would take over the world. This dynamic discomfited and alarmed elected leaders, many of whom were slave owners, and most of whom were oligarchs who had reason to identify more with the monarchs sent to the guillotines than with the middle class at the wheels of the reign of terror. The Federalists (the party of the second U.S. president, John Adams) were particularly wary of the new immigrants, for they saw the growing population as a threat comprised of individuals who had resisted ruling power back home. The Democratic-Republicans (the party of Adams's vice president, Thomas Jefferson), on the other hand, were more pro-French, and more welcoming of immigrants.

Notably, at this juncture of our democracy, the idea of political parties had not yet solidified. Indeed, leading historians consider the enactment of the Alien and Sedition Acts of 1898 and its aftermath to be a seminal point at which the two-party system grew entrenched in American politics.

The tensions in America rose when, upon Louis XVI's execution, France entered a war with Great Britain. France had been America's ally during its own revolution and hoped for reciprocal support. But President George Washington had been wary—believing that young America could ill afford a war abroad, he had demurred and declared neutrality. Tensions continued to rise during this period known as the Quasi-War, so much so that when President Adams took office, he openly contemplated the prospect of waging formal war with France. In late 1797, in an effort to quell tensions abroad and at home, Adams sent envoys to attempt to broker peace. Alas, that merely inflamed tensions further: the French foreign minister rebuffed the envoys by demanding a bribe before engaging in negotiations—a then commonplace practice, but one that enraged Americans. The incident later became popularly known as the XYZ Affair (*X, Y,* and *Z* denoting the redacted names of the French intermediaries who worked with Adams's envoys).

When news of the XYZ Affair broke, the tide of public opinion at home began to rise against the French and in Adams's and the Federalists' favor. The Federalists rode this wave into the 1798 elections, bolstering their majority in the House of Representatives. America remained a house divided: the Democratic-Republicans stayed pro-French, and in a missive to James Madison, Thomas Jefferson called Adams's dealings with France "insane." But in 1798, Philadelphia saw marches, violence, and riots led by anti-French, pro-Federalist mobs who threatened all those who disagreed—in particular, the printers of Democratic-Republican, pro-French newspapers, chief among them the Philadelphia-based *Aurora.*

Using the congressional might at their disposal, the Federalists saw the opportunity to enact laws that would quash dissent and amass power and control—especially over the

Democratic-Republicans, who advocated, inconveniently, for strong state governments, support for foreign republics, and politically engaged constituents. And so it was that the Alien and Sedition Acts came into being in July 1798.

The Federalists saw manifold threats to their reigning power: the suspect immigrant classes, with their foreign, pro-French values; the free press with its loud and dissenting journalists; and the sizeable numbers of natural-born Americans who seemed to agree with them. So, to control for each of these threats, the Federalists undertook a four-part strategy that took form in each of the acts.

First, the Naturalization Act targeted immigrants by extending the requirement for naturalization—the process by which noncitizen foreigners ("aliens") could become United States citizens—from five years of residency to a whopping fourteen years. It also moved naturalization from the domain of the states to that of the federal government and established a national registry of aliens. Second, the Alien Act (also known as the Alien Friends Act) gave the president the extraordinary power to jail and deport any immigrant suspected of being "dangerous to the peace and safety of the United States." It denied immigrants due process and the right to a fair hearing. Third, the Alien Enemies Act conferred essentially the same unfettered power on the president as did the Alien Act, but only in the event of a formally declared war. Notably, whereas the Alien Act was intended for temporary use and thus set to expire shortly, the Alien Enemies Act had no built-in expiry date. And fourth, the Sedition Act targeted citizens who dared to dissent by prohibiting them from writing or speaking critically of the president, Congress, or the government. Violation resulted in fines and imprisonment.

Although the acts were presented as necessary protections for the safety of America, they were more useful as political vehicles, designed to confer benefits upon Adams and his administration. As just an example, the Alien Friends Act and the Sedition Act expired in 1800 and 1801, respectively, with the Sedition Act expiring on the very last day of Adams's term.

III. Governance "by a Rod of Iron"

The backlash came immediately. Ten states condemned the acts as unconstitutional, and, of particular note, Thomas Jefferson drafted the Kentucky Resolutions and James Madison the Virginia Resolutions. Though Madison privately remarked to Jefferson that the set of laws was "a monster that must for ever disgrace his parents," publicly he was more reserved, simply calling upon states to oppose and fight the acts. Jefferson, on the other hand, was strident. He laid out what is now known as compact theory: the reasoning that the Constitution was formed through a compact agreed upon by all states, and that, as such, states are empowered to reject and nullify federal laws like the Alien and Sedition Acts. Jefferson went so far as to warn against the dangers that the acts posed to the very principles of democracy and justice. In his November 10, 1798, draft of the Kentucky Resolutions, he called the acts "new pretexts for those who wish it to be believed that man cannot be governed but by a rod of iron." He further declared the acts "tyranny" and cautioned: "confidence is every where the parent of despotism; free government is founded in jealousy, and not in confidence; it is jealousy, and not confidence, which prescribes limited constitutions to bind down those whom we are obliged to trust with power."

Jefferson, a slave owner, was perhaps guided by less-than-perfect morals: anti-abolitionist states subsequently used his compact theory to argue for secession just before the Civil War and, later, to resist desegregation. But the Supreme Court has repeatedly held that federal laws have supreme governance, rejecting Jefferson's constitutional framework and ruling instead for contract theory, which holds that the United States and its Constitution were formed by the consent of "we the people of the United States," not the disparate states themselves.

Even so, Jefferson's warnings about the acts were borne out. Although the Alien Act never saw constitutional challenge before it expired in 1800, it was the genesis of what would become an entrenched principle in American immigration law: permitting the deportation of aliens on vague—one might argue, unconstitutionally so—political grounds, which shift to match contemporary political agendas.

And, as the only one of the acts still in effect, the Alien Enemies Act has continued to influence American jurisprudence and governance. During the War of 1812, President James Madison resisted the temptation to pass a new sedition law, but—despite having opposed Adams at the time of its enactment—he did use the Alien Enemies Act to require British subjects to report to the government. The same anti-immigrant sentiment that gave rise to the acts led to the nation's decision to end its open borders in 1875, when Congress passed the Page Act, America's very first restrictive immigration statute. The Page Act effectively prohibited entry of Chinese women (along with women from "Japan, or any Oriental Country"), implying that all such immigrants were entering for the "purposes of prostitution" and for "lewd and immoral purposes." Just seven years later, that act would lead to the full-scale exclusion of Chinese immigrants—an exclusion that would remain entrenched in law for over six decades. Then, during World War I, Congress passed the Sedition Act of 1918 (set to expire two years later) to suppress dissent, and President Woodrow Wilson invoked the Alien Enemies Act to require registration from German and Austro-Hungarian nationals, restrict their movement, and bar them from owning firearms.

IV. World War II and Internment

None of this, however, compares to the scope of executive power exercised under the Alien Enemies Act during World War II, which saw its first use against a group singled out based on ethnicity and race instead of nationality. Hours after Japan launched its surprise attack on Pearl Harbor on December 7, 1941, the federal government began to make largely warrantless arrests of Japanese Americans, deeming them "enemy aliens" even before the formal declaration of war, which was not issued against Japan until the next day. And on December 8, 1941, even though the declaration of war against Germany would not come until days later, officials arrested German and Italian immigrants. The roundups were made in the name of protecting Americans, but Americans themselves—certainly, Japanese Americans, along with others of German and Italian descent—were the ones being held without due process.

In February 1942, President Franklin Delano Roosevelt issued an executive order formally authorizing the internment of Japanese Americans. Notably, although the order described only "residents" and "alien enemies" suspected of espionage and "sabotage to national-defense," in practice, the government only applied the order to the racial and ethnic groups they had already begun rounding up. By September 1942, over 122,000 Japanese Americans had been forcibly moved to internment camps operated by the military, along with 11,500 people of German heritage and 3,000 people of Italian heritage. Of the people of Japanese heritage sent to the camps, more than two-thirds were native-born Americans. And although internment was largely intended to target them, the exercise of power under the Alien Enemies Act stoked racist fervor across the country, so much so that other Asian Americans, including Chinese and Korean Americans, reported being stopped, detained, beaten, and threatened with internment.

Although most Japanese Americans abided by the internment order, hoping to prove their loyalty to their country and thereby earn their way to what should have been unalienable rights, some tried to dodge it. Among them was Fred Korematsu, a twenty-three-year-old man born in Oakland, California. To evade relocation, Korematsu underwent plastic surgery to change his appearance and took on a fake name. He was subsequently arrested—

despite facing no allegations of disloyalty to America, and despite his clean record—and he agreed to have the ACLU use his case to challenge the legality of Japanese internment. That case, *Korematsu v. United States,* made it all the way to the U.S. Supreme Court, resulting in a piece of American jurisprudence that lives in infamy.

The court rejected Korematsu's arguments 6–3. Authoring the majority opinion, Justice Hugo Black reasoned that the government had met the strict scrutiny test—the most stringent legal standard in constitutional law, applied to presumptively invalid legislation. Justice Black reasoned that forcibly moving 122,000 Japanese Americans was a "narrowly tailored" and "least restrictive means" of servicing a "compelling state interest"—that is, rooting out espionage. The court ruled that Korematsu had not been targeted "because of hostility to him or his race," but rather because "the military urgency of the situation demanded that all citizens of Japanese ancestry be segregated," and the court could not substitute its judgment for the military's.

Justice Frank Murphy dissented forcefully from what he called the "legalization of racism." Indeed, he warned that the internment of Japanese Americans "goes over the very brink of constitutional power," comparing it to "the abhorrent and despicable treatment of minority groups by the dictatorial tyrannies which this nation is now pledged to destroy." And in his now famous dissent, Justice Robert H. Jackson avowed that internment had "no place in law under the Constitution." He also highlighted the dangers of a decision that allowed the executive and the military to go unchecked: "We may as well say that any military order will be constitutional."

Just four years later, the dissent's strident warnings materialized and were etched further into law. In the 1948 case of *Ludecke v. Watkins*, the Supreme Court reviewed the case of Kurt Ludecke, a German national against whom the government had invoked the Alien Enemies Act, ordering him to be deported without fair hearing after Germany had already surrendered. Representing himself before the high court, Ludecke argued that the Alien Enemies Act could no longer be invoked, because it explicitly pertained to wartime. Ruling 5–4, the court rejected that argument, further extending the powers of the president under the act. Writing for the majority, Justice Felix Frankfurter invoked the political question doctrine, which holds that some issues by their nature are fundamentally political and are therefore unreviewable by the courts. Noting the "very great discretionary powers" that the act confers upon the president, the court reasoned that, other than interpretative and constitutional issues, the judiciary could not rule upon challenges to the Alien Enemies Act.

As for the wartime limitation, the court reasoned that restricting the president to invoking the act during wartime "nullifies the power to deport alien enemies," because deportations are "hardly practicable during the pendency of what is colloquially known as the shooting war." The court endorsed an expanded (and again one could argue, an unconstitutionally vague) definition of wartime, suggesting that even when wars have technically ended, the president may continue to wield the expansive powers accorded by the Alien Enemies Act. Citing President Truman's Proclamation 2714, titled Cessation of Hostilities of World War II, the court pointed to evidence that "the political branch has not brought the war with Germany to an end." (In that proclamation, Truman clearly declares "the cessation of hostilities of World War II, effective twelve o'clock noon, December 31, 1946," but the court instead focused on the sentence that states in passing: "Although a state of war still exists, it is at this time possible to declare . . . that hostilities have terminated.") The majority closed by granting virtually unfettered power to the president: "The Founders in their wisdom made him not only the Commander-in-Chief but also the guiding organ in the conduct of our foreign affairs. He who was entrusted with such vast powers in relation to the outside world was also entrusted by Congress, almost throughout the whole life of the nation, with the disposition of alien enemies during a state of war. Such a page of history is worth more than a volume of rhetoric." In this way, *Ludecke* expanded the Alien Enemies Act to such breadth that it gave the president nearly as much expansive discretion as that accorded by the short-lived Alien Act.

Dissenting this time, Justice Black warned that, for the first time, the government and the court alike were permitting removal of immigrants without fair hearing. Such erosion of due process meant that "because of today's opinion, individual liberty will be less secure tomorrow than it was yesterday." Similarly, Justice William Douglas observed that "it is undisputed that in peacetime an alien is protected by the due process clause of the Fifth Amendment." Nor could wartime erase American legal safeguards: "The notion that the discretion of any officer of government can override due process is foreign to our system. Due process does not perish when war comes. It is well established that the war power does not remove constitutional limitations safeguarding essential liberties."

V. "Less Secure Than . . . Yesterday"

At the time of this writing, our country is witnessing the most expansive usage of the Alien Enemies Act yet: almost immediately after taking office for his second term, President Donald Trump started to test the limits of his discretionary powers during peacetime. In the spirit of the Alien Enemies Act, which targeted politically subversive immigrants, the Trump administration quickly began to detain and threaten to deport numerous noncitizens who had spoken out against the United States' financing of Israel's genocide in Gaza. Then, on March 15, 2025, absent any declaration of war, imminent or otherwise, President Trump issued a proclamation explicitly invoking the Alien Enemies Act against those allegedly involved with Tren de Aragua, a gang that the president claimed was sponsored by the Nicolás Maduro regime in Venezuela. Echoing its actions in the hours following Pearl Harbor, the federal government did not wait for this announcement before rounding up and deporting scores of individuals who they claimed—in some cases, incorrectly—were affiliated with Tren de Aragua. (Months later, the government announced a new large scale immigration detention facility called "Alligator Alcatraz," quickly eliciting media comparisons to

Japanese internment camps and Nazi concentration camps.) The president moved so quickly that courts across the nation had to issue temporary restraining orders the very same day, but even that was not swift enough. In violation of court orders and under cover of night, the administration preloaded planes with deportees and waited to publish President Trump's proclamation until just minutes before the first planes were set to take off for El Salvador. By the time one of the expedited cases made its way up to the Supreme Court three weeks later, the administration had already deported over two hundred people; by the government's own admission, at least one, Kilmar Armando Abrego Garcia, had been wrongly deported.

The court issued its first decision in *Trump v. J.G.G.* on April 7, 2025. Ruling per curiam—that is, in a decision format generally intended to resolve noncontroversial cases in a speedy and unanimous fashion, though in this instance four justices dissented—the court once again reasoned that presidential discretion under the Alien Enemies Act could not be judicially reviewed. As a preliminary matter, the majority decision dodged the specious invocation of the act, which explicitly confers presidential powers only "whenever there shall be a declared war between the United States *and any foreign nation or government*, or any invasion or predatory incursion shall be perpetrated, attempted, or threatened against the territory of the United States, *by any foreign nation or government*" (Alien Enemies Act, section 1, emphasis added). In addition to holding, as it had in *Ludecke*, that challenges to deportations under the act "largely preclude judicial review," the court went further to hold that such cases—unreviewable as they are—must further be brought in separate habeas corpus actions by each detainee in the federal courts with jurisdiction over their place of detention.

Habeas protects against indefinite detention or imprisonment without due process; it offers a particular mechanism through which prisoners and detainees may bring legal challenges. The court did clarify that detainees under the act were entitled to notice that they are subject to removal and, as in *Ludecke,* it stated that judges can review "questions of interpretation and constitutionality," as well as whether a certain individual qualifies as an enemy under the act. Even so, the court reversed the temporary restraining order on technical grounds because the case was brought in the wrong legal manner. The decision makes no mention of section 2 of the act, which clearly states that prior to ordering the deportation, the president is required to first make the alien available to courts of competent jurisdiction and afford "a full examination and hearing" to establish "sufficient cause" for removal—legal procedure that the Trump administration flagrantly ignored.

Once again, the dissents raged. Justice Sonia Sotomayor pointed out the precious toll—"the scores of individual lives that may be irretrievably lost"—of the federal government's staunch resistance to returning even the individuals they admitted to having wrongly deported. She further cautioned: "The implication of the Government's position is that not only noncitizens but also United States citizens could be taken off the streets, forced into planes, and confined to foreign prisons with no opportunity for redress if judicial review is denied unlawfully before removal. History is no stranger to such lawless regimes, but this Nation's system of laws is designed to prevent, not enable, their rise."

VI. The Path Forward, Guided by Roads Traveled

Justice Sotomayor's gesture toward history is an apt one. It is this very descent into unchecked executive power that the Alien and Sedition Acts' earliest opponents warned against. It cannot be ignored that each invocation of the Alien Enemies Act has caused irrevocable harm to countless lives—human lives that will never be made whole, no matter the redress after the fact. Even so, current circumstances, as well as past history, offer some rays of light.

Shortly after midnight on Saturday, April 19, 2025—twelve days after ruling that courts could not intervene in *J.G.G.*—the Supreme Court issued a terse order forbidding President Trump from further deportations of the individuals at issue. Less than a month later, on May 16, 2025, the court followed up with another per curiam decision, this time with only two dissenters, reversing a lower court's dismissal of another related case under the Alien Enemies Act and imposing once again stays of deportation to allow time for courts across the country to issue decisions. In so doing, the court highlighted that the Trump administration gave the detainees mere hours' notice—indicating that they would be deported "tonight or tomorrow"—and had admitted to being "unable to provide for the return of an individual deported in error to a prison in El Salvador, where it is alleged that detainees face indefinite detention." Echoing Justice Douglas's dissent in *Ludecke*, the court made clear that "the Fifth Amendment entitles aliens to due process of law in the context of removal proceedings," that procedural due process is designed to "protect against the mistaken or unjustified deprivation of life, liberty, or property," and that the court's jurisprudence provided that "no person shall be removed from the United States without opportunity, at some time, to be heard."

Though it often comes less swiftly, and though it does little to repair the harms already inflicted, this kind of reversal is not the first in our nation's history. *Ludecke* certainly established broad and dangerous presidential powers, but it still permitted constitutional review of the Alien Enemies Act—review that can and should take place in the years to come. And the Supreme Court has since installed some limits on detention: its 2001 decision in *Zadvydas v. Davis* clearly established a constitutional right to be free from indefinite detention under civil laws—a right that the court recognized, if reluctantly, in its early 2025 decisions pertaining to the act.

Delayed justice also eventually found the hundreds of thousands of Japanese Americans who were sent to military camps overnight. Their internment is widely recognized as among the darkest chapters in American history. After the passage of the Civil Liberties Act of 1988, President George H. W. Bush signed formal letters of apology to some sixty thousand survivors, who also received $20,000 each in compensation, a meager sum in light of the rights violated, the property lost, and the injuries that cannot be undone. The government never did turn up any evidence of espionage or threats posed by Japanese Americans. In fact, despite America's mistreatment of them as perpetual foreigners, some thirty-three thousand Japanese Americans joined the U.S. Army in World War II, serving in the segregated 100th Infantry Battalion and the 442nd Infantry Regiment. They fought in Italy, liberated Rome, and endured horrific casualties for their country, with some eight hundred killed in action. They quickly earned esteem, and the 100th Infantry Battalion would go on to become the most decorated unit in U.S. military history.

Korematsu's conviction was overturned in 1983, when the federal court and the acting solicitor general recognized publicly that the government had suppressed critical evidence that would have exonerated him. The Supreme Court has since overruled its decision in *Korematsu v. United States*, declaring in 2018, with a quote from Justice Jackson's dissent: "*Korematsu* was gravely wrong the day it was decided, has been overruled in the court of history, and—to be clear—'has no place in law under the Constitution.'"

As for the original Alien and Sedition Acts, John Adams lived to regret their creation, reflecting in a letter to his son, "I regret not the repeal of the Alien or the Sedition Law, which were never favorites with me." The acts lost Adams and his party popular favor, and Thomas Jefferson would go on to win the 1800 election just two years later. The Alien Act was never invoked, and no one was ever deported under it; and while ten individuals were convicted under the Sedition Act, most of them editors of Democratic-Republican newspapers, the convictions backfired. Before the acts passed, the government arrested the editor of the *Aurora*, and the Senate held him in contempt. He posted bail and would die of yellow fever before he could be tried, but the *Aurora* lived on, continuing in print for over two decades after the Sedition Act expired. The Federalists won every sedition trial, but each win cost them the very purpose of those trials—muting dissent—for each courtroom drama gave the "seditious" the ideal platform for their claims. Those jailed for sedition garnered fame and, later, political power: one newspaper printer established a new magazine featuring his letters from jail, and another courted arrest so that he could publish his own account of the trial during the height of the 1800 presidential race, which catapulted him into politics. If Trump and future presidents learn anything from the Federalists, it should be that dissent is a fire, and attempts to silence it only fan the flames, emboldening them to burn brighter.

When Jefferson won the election of 1800, he quickly pardoned all those convicted for sedition, and Congress refunded their fines. The Democratic-Republicans also quickly reduced the naturalization requirement back to five years and restored to the states oversight of naturalization. An American reading the legal headlines in 1802 might have been excused for believing that all was well that ended well.

But the bell—whether of liberty or oppression—cannot be unrung. The Alien Enemies Act warns us that the bedrock of our democracy is more porous than we'd like to believe. The history of the acts teaches that if rights are conditional for one of us, they are conditional for all of us. Some two hundred years later, Jefferson's words—"confidence is every where the parent of despotism"—still ring true, reminding us that we must never take democracy for granted, forget that it is a most precarious thing. America errs and America falters, but she is our nation, and one ever reaching for the vision of liberty and justice that lies just beyond the horizon. Our nation's history calls upon us to serve as jealous guards. It is our responsibility to make sure that America forever has the means to correct herself. For if the Constitution was formed by the free will and consent of "we the people," it is we the people who must demand that our nation live up to her loftiest ideals.

—

QIAN JULIE WANG is the author of the *New York Times* bestseller *Beautiful Country: A Memoir of an Undocumented Childhood.* A graduate of Yale Law School and Swarthmore College, she was formerly a commercial litigator and is now managing partner of Gottlieb & Wang LLP, a firm dedicated to advocating for education and civil rights. Her writing has appeared in publications such as *The New York Times* and *The Washington Post.* She lives in Brooklyn, New York, with her family.

I.

The Alien and Sedition Acts

The Naturalization Act of 1798

An Act supplementary to and to amend the act, intituled "An act to establish an uniform rule of naturalization; and to repeal the act heretofore passed on that subject."

SECTION 1. *Be it enacted by the Senate and House of Representatives of the United States of America in Congress assembled,* That no alien shall be admitted to become a citizen of the United States, or of any state, unless in the manner prescribed by the act, intituled "An act to establish an uniform rule of naturalization; and to repeal the act heretofore passed on that subject," he shall have declared his intention to become a citizen of the United States, five years, at least, before his admission, and shall, at the time of his application to be admitted, declare and prove, to the satisfaction of the court having jurisdiction in the case, that he has resided within the United States fourteen years, at least, and within the state or territory where, or for which such court is at the time held, five years, at least, besides conforming to the other declarations, renunciations and proofs, by the said act required, any thing therein to the contrary hereof notwithstanding: *Provided,* that any alien, who was residing within the limits, and under the jurisdiction of the United States, before the twenty-ninth day of January, one thousand seven hundred and ninety-five, may, within one year after the passing of this act—and any alien who shall have made the declaration of his intention to become a citizen of the United States, in conformity to the provisions of the act, intituled "An act to establish an uniform rule of naturalization, and to repeal the act heretofore passed on that subject," may, within four years after having made the declaration aforesaid, be admitted to become a citizen, in the manner prescribed by the said act, upon his making proof that he has resided five years, at least, within the limits, and under the jurisdiction of the United States: *And provided also,* that no alien, who shall be a native, citizen, denizen or subject of any nation or state with whom the United States shall be at war, at the time of his application, shall be then admitted to become a citizen of the United States.

SEC. 2. *And be it further enacted,* That it shall be the duty of the clerk, or other recording officer of the court before whom a declaration has been, or shall be made, by any alien, of his intention to become a citizen of the United States, to certify and transmit to the office of the Secretary of State of the United States, to be there filed and recorded, an abstract of such declaration, in which, when hereafter made, shall be a suitable description of the name, age, nation, residence and occupation, for the time being, of the alien; such certificate to be made in all cases, where the declaration has been or shall be made, before the passing of this act, within three months thereafter; and in all other cases, within two months after the declaration shall be received by the court. And in all cases hereafter arising, there shall be paid to the clerk, or recording officer as aforesaid, to defray the expense of such abstract and certificate, a fee of two dollars; and the clerk or officer to whom such fee shall be paid or tendered, who shall refuse or neglect to make and certify an abstract, as aforesaid, shall forfeit and pay the sum of ten dollars.

SEC. 3. *And be it further enacted,* That in all cases of naturalization heretofore permitted or which shall be permitted, under the laws of the United States, a certificate shall be made to, and filed in the office of the Secretary of State, containing a copy of the record respecting the alien, and the decree or order of admission by the court before whom the proceedings thereto have been, or shall be had: And it shall be the duty of the clerk or other recording officer of such court, to make and transmit such certificate, in all cases which have already occurred, within three months after the passing of this act; and in all future cases, within two months from and after the naturalization of an alien shall be granted by any court competent thereto:—And in all future cases, there shall be paid to such clerk or recording officer the sum of two dollars, as a fee for such certificate, before the naturalization prayed for, shall be allowed. And the clerk or recording officer, whose duty it shall be, to make and transmit the certificate aforesaid, who shall be convicted of a wilful neglect therein, shall forfeit and pay the sum of ten dollars, for each and every offence.

SEC. 4. *And be it further enacted,* That all white persons, aliens, (accredited foreign ministers, consuls, or agents, their families and domestics, excepted) who, after the passing of this act, shall continue to reside, or who shall arrive, or come to reside in any port or place within the territory of the United States, shall be reported, if free, and of the age of twenty-one years, by themselves, or being under the age of twenty-one years, or holden in service, by their parent, guardian, master or mistress in whose care they shall be, to the clerk of the district court of the district, if living within ten miles of the port or place, in which their residence or arrival shall be, and otherwise, to the collector of such port or place, or some officer or other person there, or nearest thereto, who shall be authorized by the President of the United States, to register aliens: And report, as aforesaid, shall be made in all cases of residence, within six months from and after the passing of this act, and in all after cases, within forty-eight hours after the first arrival or coming into the territory of the United States, and shall ascertain the sex, place of birth, age, nation, place of allegiance or citizenship, condition or occupation, and place of actual or intended residence within the United States, of the alien or aliens reported, and by whom the report is made. And it shall be the duty of the clerk, or other officer, or person authorized, who shall receive such report, to record the same in a book to be kept for that purpose, and to grant to the person making the report, and to each individual concerned therein, whenever required, a certificate of such report and registry; and whenever such report and registry shall be made to, and by any officer or person authorized, as aforesaid, other than the clerk of the district court, it shall be the duty of such officer, or other person, to certify and transmit, within three months thereafter, a transcript of such registry, to the said clerk of the district court of the district in which the same shall happen; who shall file the same in his office, and shall enter and transcribe the same in a book to be kept by him for that purpose. And the clerk, officer or other person authorized to register aliens, shall be entitled to receive, for each report and registry of one individual or family of individuals, the sum of fifty cents, and for every certificate of a report and registry the sum of fifty cents, to be paid by the person making or requiring the same, respectively. And the clerk of the district court, to whom a return of the registry of any alien, shall have been made, as aforesaid, and the successor of such clerk, and of any other officer or person authorized to register aliens, who shall hold any former registry, shall and may grant certificates thereof, to the same effect as the original register might do. And the clerk of each district court shall, during one year from the passing of this act, make monthly returns to the department of State, of all aliens registered and returned, as aforesaid, in his office.

SEC. 5. *And be it further enacted,* That every alien who shall continue to reside, or who shall arrive, as aforesaid, of whom a report is required as aforesaid, who shall refuse or neglect to make such report, and to receive a certificate thereof, shall forfeit and pay the sum of two dollars; and any justice of the peace, or other civil magistrate, who has authority to require surety of the peace, shall and may, on complaint to him made thereof, cause such alien to be brought before him, there to give surety of the peace and good behaviour during his residence within the United States, or for such term as the justice or other magistrate shall deem reasonable, and until a report and registry of such alien shall be made, and a certificate thereof, received as aforesaid; and in failure of such surety, such alien shall and may be committed to the common gaol, and shall be there held, until the order which the justice or magistrate shall and may reasonably make, in the premises, shall be performed. And every person, whether alien, or other, having the care of any alien or aliens, under the age of twenty-one years, or of any white alien holden in service, who shall refuse and neglect to make report thereof, as aforesaid, shall forfeit the sum of two dollars, for each and every such minor or servant, monthly, and every month, until a report and registry, and a certificate thereof, shall be had, as aforesaid.

SEC. 6. *And be it further enacted,* That in respect to every alien, who shall come to reside within the United States after the passing of this act, the time of the registry of such alien shall be taken to be the time when the term of residence within the limits, and under the jurisdiction of the United States, shall have commenced, in case of an application by such alien, to be admitted a citizen of the United States; and a certificate of such registry shall be required, in proof of the term of residence, by the court to whom such application shall and may be made.

SEC. 7. *And be it further enacted,* That all and singular the penalties established by this act, shall and may be recovered in the name, and to the use of any person, who will inform and sue for the same, before any judge, justice, or court, having jurisdiction in such case, and to the amount of such penalty, respectively.

APPROVED, June 18, 1798.

The Alien Act

An Act concerning aliens.

SECTION 1. *Be it enacted by the Senate and the House of Representatives of the United States of America in Congress assembled,* That it shall be lawful for the President of the United States at any time during the continuance of this act, to order all such aliens as he shall judge dangerous to the peace and safety of the United States, or shall have reasonable grounds to suspect are concerned in any treasonable or secret machinations against the government thereof, to depart out of the territory of the United States, within such time as shall be expressed in such order, which order shall be served on such alien by delivering him a copy thereof, or leaving the same at his usual abode, and returned to the office of the Secretary of State, by the marshal or other person to whom the same shall be directed. And in case any alien, so ordered to depart, shall be found at large within the United States after the time limited in such order for his departure, and not having obtained a license from the President to reside therein, or having obtained such license shall not have conformed thereto, every such alien shall, on conviction thereof, be imprisoned for a term not exceeding three years, and shall never after be admitted to become a citizen of the United States. Provided always, and be it further enacted, that if any alien so ordered to depart shall prove to the satisfaction of the President, by evidence to be taken before such person or persons as the President shall direct, who are for that purpose hereby authorized to administer oaths, that no injury or danger to the United States will arise from suffering such alien to reside therein, the President may grant a license to such alien to remain within the United States for such time as he shall judge proper, and at such place as he may designate. And the President may also require of such alien to enter into a bond to the United States, in such penal sum as he may direct, with one or more sufficient sureties to the satisfaction of the person authorized by the President to take the same, conditioned for the good behavior of such alien during his residence in the United States, and not violating his license, which license the President may revoke, whenever he shall think proper.

SEC. 2. *And be it further enacted,* That it shall be lawful for the President of the United States, whenever he may deem it necessary for the public safety, to order to be removed out of the territory thereof, any alien who may or shall be in prison in pursuance of this act; and to cause to be arrested and sent out of the United States such of those aliens as shall have been ordered to depart therefrom and shall not have obtained a license as aforesaid, in all cases where, in the opinion of the President, the public safety requires a speedy removal. And if any alien so removed or sent out of the United States by the President shall voluntarily return thereto, unless by permission of the President of the United States, such alien on conviction thereof, shall be imprisoned so long as, in the opinion of the President, the public safety may require.

SEC. 3. *And be it further enacted,* That every master or commander of any ship or vessel which shall come into any port of the United States after the first day of July next, shall immediately on his arrival make report in writing to the collector or other chief officer of the customs of such port, of all aliens, if any, on board his vessel, specifying their names, age, the place of nativity, the country from which they shall have come, the nation to which they belong and owe allegiance, their occupation and a description of their persons, as far as he shall be informed thereof, and on failure, every such master and commander shall forfeit and pay three hundred dollars, for the payment whereof on default of such master or commander, such vessel shall also be holden, and may by such collector or other officer of the customs be detained. And it shall be the duty of such collector or other officer of the customs, forthwith to transmit to the office of the Department of State true copies of all such returns.

SEC. 4. *And be it further enacted,* That the circuit and district courts of the United States, shall respectively have cognizance of all crimes and offences against this act. And all marshals and other officers of the United States are required to execute all precepts and orders of the President of the United States issued in pursuance or by virtue of this act.

SEC. 5. *And be it further enacted,* That it shall be lawful for any alien who may be ordered to be removed from the United States, by virtue of this act, to take with him such part of his goods, chattels, or other property, as he may find convenient; and all property left in the United States by any alien, who may be removed, as aforesaid, shall be, and remain subject to his order and disposal, in the same manner as if this act had not been passed.

SEC. 6. *And be it further enacted,* That this act shall continue and be in force for and during the term of two years from the passing thereof.

APPROVED, June 25, 1798.

THE ALIEN ENEMIES ACT

An Act respecting alien enemies.

SECTION I. *Be it enacted by the Senate and House of Representatives of the United States of America in Congress assembled,* That whenever there shall be a declared war between the United States and any foreign nation or government, or any invasion or predatory incursion shall be perpetrated, attempted, or threatened against the territory of the United States, by any foreign nation or government, and the President of the United States shall make public proclamation of the event, all natives, citizens, denizens, or subjects of the hostile nation or government, being males of the age of fourteen years and upwards, who shall be within the United States, and not actually naturalized, shall be liable to be apprehended, restrained, secured and removed, as alien enemies. And the President of the United States shall be, and he is hereby authorized, in any event, as aforesaid, by his proclamation thereof, or other public act, to direct the conduct to be observed, on the part of the United States, towards the aliens who shall become liable, as aforesaid; the manner and degree of the restraint to which they shall be subject, and in what cases, and upon what security their residence shall be permitted, and to provide for the removal of those, who, not being permitted to reside within the United States, shall refuse or neglect to depart therefrom; and to establish any other regulations which shall be found necessary in the premises and for the public safety: Provided, that aliens resident within the United States, who shall become liable as enemies, in the manner aforesaid, and who shall not be chargeable with actual hostility, or other crime against the public safety, shall be allowed, for the recovery, disposal, and removal of their goods and effects, and for their departure, the full time which is, or shall be stipulated by any treaty, where any shall have been between the United States, and the hostile nation or government, of which they shall be natives, citizens, denizens or subjects: and where no such treaty shall have existed, the President of the United States may ascertain and declare such reasonable time as may be consistent with the public safety, and according to the dictates of humanity and national hospitality.

SEC. 2. *And be it further enacted,* That after any proclamation shall be made as aforesaid, it shall be the duty of the several courts of the United States, and of each state, having criminal jurisdiction, and of the several judges and justices of the courts of the United States, and they shall be, and are hereby respectively, authorized upon complaint, against any alien or alien enemies, as aforesaid, who shall be resident and at large within such jurisdiction or district, to the danger of the public peace or safety, and contrary to the tenor or intent of such proclamation, or other regulations which the President of the United States shall and may establish in the premises, to cause such alien or aliens to be duly apprehended and convened before such court, judge or justice; and after a full examination and hearing on such complaint, and sufficient cause therefor appearing, shall and may order such alien or aliens to be removed out of the territory of the United States, or to give sureties of their good behaviour, or to be otherwise restrained, conformably to the proclamation or regulations which shall and may be established as aforesaid, and may imprison, or otherwise secure such alien or aliens, until the order which shall and may be made, as aforesaid, shall be performed.

SEC. 3. *And be it further enacted,* That it shall be the duty of the marshal of the district in which any alien enemy shall be apprehended, who by the President of the United States, or by order of any court, judge or justice, as aforesaid, shall be required to depart, and to be removed, as aforesaid, to provide therefor, and to execute such order, by himself or his deputy, or other discreet person or persons to be employed by him, by causing a removal of such alien out of the territory of the United States; and for such removal the marshal shall have the warrant of the President of the United States, or of the court, judge or justice ordering the same, as the case may be.

APPROVED, July 6, 1798.

The Sedition Act

An Act in addition to the act, entitled "An Act for the punishment of certain crimes against the United States."

SECTION 1. *Be it enacted by the Senate and House of Representatives of the United States of America, in Congress assembled,* That if any persons shall unlawfully combine or conspire together, with intent to oppose any measure or measures of the government of the United States, which are or shall be directed by proper authority, or to impede the operation of any law of the United States, or to intimidate or prevent any person holding a place or office in or under the government of the United States, from undertaking, performing or executing his trust or duty, and if any person or persons, with intent as aforesaid, shall counsel, advise or attempt to procure any insurrection, riot, unlawful assembly, or combination, whether such conspiracy, threatening, counsel, advice, or attempt shall have the proposed effect or not, he or they shall be deemed guilty of a high misdemeanor, and on conviction, before any court of the United States having jurisdiction thereof, shall be punished by a fine not exceeding five thousand dollars, and by imprisonment during a term not less than six months nor exceeding five years; and further, at the discretion of the court may be holden to find sureties for his good behaviour in such sum, and for such time, as the said court may direct.

SEC. 2. *And be it further enacted,* That if any person shall write, print, utter or publish, or shall cause or procure to be written, printed, uttered or published, or shall knowingly and willingly assist or aid in writing, printing, uttering or publishing any false, scandalous and malicious writing or writings against the government of the United States, or either house of the Congress of the United States, or the President of the United States, with intent to defame the said government, or either house of the said Congress, or the said President, or to bring them, or either of them, into contempt or disrepute; or to excite against them, or either or any of them, the hatred of the good people of the United States, or to stir up sedition within the United States, or to excite any unlawful combinations therein, for opposing or resisting any law of the United States, or any act of the President of the United States, done in pursuance of any such law, or of the powers in him vested by the Constitution of the United States, or to resist, oppose, or defeat any such law or act, or to aid, encourage or abet any hostile designs of any foreign nation against United States, their people or government, then such person, being thereof convicted before any court of the United States having jurisdiction thereof, shall be punished by a fine not exceeding two thousand dollars, and by imprisonment not exceeding two years.

SEC. 3. *And be it further enacted and declared,* That if any person shall be prosecuted under this act, for the writing or publishing any libel aforesaid, it shall be lawful for the defendant, upon the trial of the cause, to give in evidence in his defence, the truth of the matter contained in publication charged as a libel. And the jury who shall try the cause, shall have a right to determine the law and the fact, under the direction of the court, as in other cases.

SEC. 4. *And be it further enacted,* That this act shall continue and be in force until the third day of March, one thousand eight hundred and one, and no longer: Provided, that the expiration of the act shall not prevent or defeat a prosecution and punishment of any offence against the law, during the time it shall be in force.

APPROVED, July 14, 1798.

II.
Resolutions

The Kentucky Resolutions of 1798

The original draft prepared by Thomas Jefferson.

The following Resolutions passed the House of Representatives of Kentucky, Nov. 10, 1798. On the passage of the 1st Resolution, one dissentient; 2d, 3d, 4th, 5th, 6th, 7th, 8th, two dissentients; 9th, three dissentients.

1. *Resolved,* That the several states composing the United States of America are not united on the principle of unlimited submission to their general government; but that, by compact, under the style and title of a Constitution for the United States, and of amendments thereto, they constituted a general government for special purposes, delegated to that government certain definite powers, reserving, each state to itself, the residuary mass of right to their own self-government; and that whensoever the general government assumes undelegated powers, its acts are unauthoritative,

void, and of no force; that to this compact each state acceded as a state, and is an integral party; that this government, created by this compact, was not made the exclusive or final judge of the extent of the powers delegated to itself, since that would have made its discretion, and not the Constitution, the measure of its powers; but that, as in all other cases of compact among parties having no common judge, *each party has an equal right to judge for itself, as well of infractions as of the mode and measure of redress.*

2. *Resolved,* That the Constitution of the United States having delegated to Congress a power to punish treason, counterfeiting the securities and current coin of the United States, piracies and felonies committed on the high seas, and offences against the laws of nations, and no other crimes whatever; and it being true, as a general principle, and one of the amendments to the Constitution having also declared "that the powers not delegated to the United States by the Constitution, nor prohibited by it to the states, are reserved to the states respectively, or to the people,"—therefore, also, the same act of Congress, passed on the 14th day of July, 1798, and entitled "An Act in Addition to the Act entitled 'An Act for the Punishment of certain Crimes against the United States;'" as also the act passed by them on the 27th day of June, 1798, entitled "An Act to punish Frauds committed on the Bank of the United States," (and all other their acts which assume to create, define, or punish crimes other than those enumerated in the Constitution,) are altogether void, and of no force; and that the power to create, define, and punish, such other crimes is reserved, and of right appertains, solely and ex-

clusively, to the respective states, each within its own territory.

3. *Resolved,* That it is true, as a general principle, and is also expressly declared by one of the amendments to the Constitution, that "the powers not delegated to the United States by the Constitution, nor prohibited by it to the states, are reserved to the states respectively, or to the people;" and that, no power over the freedom of religion, freedom of speech, or freedom of the press, being delegated to the United States by the Constitution, nor prohibited by it to the states, all lawful powers respecting the same did of right remain, and were reserved to the states, or to the people; that thus was manifested their determination to retain to themselves the right of judging how far the licentiousness of speech, and of the press, may be abridged without lessening their useful freedom, and how far those abuses which cannot be separated from their use, should be tolerated rather than the use be destroyed; and thus also they guarded against all abridgment, by the United States, of the freedom of religious principles and exercises, and retained to themselves the right of protecting the same, as this, stated by a law passed on the general demand of its citizens, had already protected them from all human restraint or interference; and that, in addition to this general principle and express declaration, another and more special provision has been made by one of the amendments to the Constitution, which expressly declares, that "Congress shall make no laws respecting an establishment of religion, or prohibiting the free exercise thereof, or abridging the freedom of speech, or of the press," thereby guarding, in

the same sentence, and under the same words, the freedom of religion, of speech, and of the press, insomuch that whatever violates either throws down the sanctuary which covers the others,—and that libels, falsehood, and defamation, equally with heresy and false religion, are withheld from the cognizance of federal tribunals. That therefore the act of the Congress of the United States, passed on the 14th of July, 1798, entitled "An Act in Addition to the Act entitled 'An Act for the Punishment of certain Crimes against the United States,'" which does abridge the freedom of the press, is not law, but is altogether void, and of no force.

4. *Resolved,* That alien friends are under the jurisdiction and protection of the laws of the state wherein they are; that no power over them has been delegated to the United States, nor prohibited to the individual states, distinct from their power over citizens; and it being true, as a general principle, and one of the amendments to the Constitution having also declared, that "the powers not delegated to the United States by the Constitution, nor prohibited to the states, are reserved, to the states, respectively, or to the people," the act of the Congress of the United States, passed the 22d day of June, 1798, entitled "An Act concerning Aliens," which assumes power over alien friends not delegated by the Constitution, is not law, but is altogether void and of no force.

5. *Resolved,* That, in addition to the general principle, as well as the express declaration, that powers not delegated are reserved, another and more special provision inserted in the Constitution from abundant caution, has declared, "that the migration or importation of such persons as any

of the states now existing shall think proper to admit, shall not be prohibited by the Congress prior to the year 1808." That this commonwealth does admit the migration of alien friends described as the subject of the said act concerning aliens; that a provision against prohibiting their migration is a provision against all acts equivalent thereto, or it would be nugatory; that to remove them, when migrated, is equivalent to a prohibition of their migration, and is, therefore, contrary to the said provision of the Constitution, and *void.*

6. *Resolved,* That the imprisonment of a person under the protection of the laws of this commonwealth, on his failure to obey the simple order of the President to depart out of the United States, as is undertaken by the said act, entitled, "An Act concerning Aliens," is contrary to the Constitution, one amendment in which has provided, that "no person shall be deprived of liberty without due process of law;" and that another having provided, "that, in all criminal prosecutions, the accused shall enjoy the right of a public trial by an impartial jury, to be informed as to the nature and cause of the accusation, to be confronted with the witnesses against him, to have compulsory process for obtaining witnesses in his favor, and to have assistance of counsel for his defence," the same act undertaking to authorize the President to remove a person out of the United States who is under the protection of the law, on his own suspicion, without jury, without public trial, without confrontation of the witnesses against him, without having witnesses in his favor, without defence, without counsel—contrary to these provisions also of the Constitution—is therefore not law, but utterly void, and of no force.

That transferring the power of judging any person who

is under the protection of the laws, from the courts to the President of the United States, as is undertaken by the same act concerning aliens, is against the article of the Constitution which provides, that "the judicial power of the United States shall be vested in the courts, the judges of which shall hold their office during good behavior," and that the said act is void for that reason also; and it is further to be noted that this transfer of judiciary power is to that magistrate of the general government who already possesses all the executive, and a qualified negative in all the legislative powers.

7. *Resolved,* That the construction applied by the general government (as is evident by sundry of their proceedings) to those parts of the Constitution of the United States which delegate to Congress power to lay and collect taxes, duties, imposts, excises; to pay the debts, and provide for the common defence and general welfare, of the United States, and to make all laws which shall be necessary and proper for carrying into execution the powers vested by the Constitution in the government of the United States, or any department thereof, goes to the destruction of all the limits prescribed to their power by the Constitution; that words meant by that instrument to be subsidiary only to the execution of the limited powers, ought not to be so construed as themselves to give unlimited powers, nor a part so to be taken as to destroy the whole residue of the instrument; that the proceedings of the general government, under color of those articles, will be a fit and necessary subject for revisal and correction at a time of greater tranquillity, while those specified in the preceding resolutions call for immediate redress.

8. *Resolved,* That the preceding resolutions be transmitted to the senators and representatives in Congress from this commonwealth, who are enjoined to present the same to their respective houses, and to use their best endeavors to procure, at the next session of Congress, a repeal of the aforesaid unconstitutional and obnoxious acts.

9. *Resolved,* lastly, That the governor of this commonwealth be, and is, authorized and requested to communicate the preceding resolutions to the legislatures of the several states, to assure them that this commonwealth considers union for special national purposes, and particularly for those specified in their late federal compact, to be friendly to the peace, happiness, and prosperity, of all the states; that, faithful to that compact, according to the plain intent and meaning in which it was understood and acceded to by the several parties, it is sincerely anxious for its preservation; that it does also believe, that, to take from the states all the powers of self-government, and transfer them to a general and consolidated government, without regard to the special government, and reservations solemnly agreed to in that compact, is not for the peace, happiness, or prosperity of these states; and that, therefore, this commonwealth is determined, as it doubts not its co-states are, to submit to undelegated and consequently unlimited powers in no man, or body of men, on earth; that, if the acts before specified should stand, these conclusions would flow from them—that the general government may place any act they think proper on the list of crimes, and punish it themselves, whether enumerated or not enumerated by the Constitution as cognizable by them; that they may transfer its cognizance to the President, or any other person, who may

himself be the accuser, counsel, judge, and jury, whose suspicions may be the evidence, his order the sentence, his officer the executioner, and his breast the sole record of the transaction; that a very numerous and valuable description of the inhabitants of these states, being, by this precedent, reduced, as outlaws, to absolute dominion of one man, and the barriers of the Constitution thus swept from us all, no rampart now remains against the passions and the power of a majority of Congress, to protect from a like exportation, or other grievous punishment, the minority of the same body, the legislatures, judges, governors, and counsellors of the states, nor their other peaceable inhabitants, who may venture to reclaim the constitutional rights and liberties of the states and people, or who, for other causes, good or bad, may be obnoxious to the view, or marked by the suspicions, of the President, or be thought dangerous to his or their elections, or other interests, public or personal; that the friendless alien has been selected as the safest subject of a first experiment; but the citizen will soon follow, or rather has already followed; for already has a Sedition Act marked him as a prey: That these and successive acts of the same character, unless arrested on the threshold, may tend to drive these states into revolution and blood, and will furnish new calumnies against republican governments, and new pretexts for those who wish it to be believed that man cannot be governed but by a rod of iron; that it would be a dangerous delusion were a confidence in the men of our choice to silence our fears for the safety of our rights; that confidence is every where the parent of despotism; free government is founded in jealousy, and not in confidence;

it is jealousy, and not confidence, which prescribes limited constitutions to bind down those whom we are obliged to trust with power; that our Constitution has accordingly fixed the limits to which, and no farther, our confidence may go; and let the honest advocate of confidence read the Alien and Sedition Acts, and say if the Constitution has not been wise in fixing limits to the government it created, and whether we should be wise in destroying those limits; let him say what the government is, if it be not a tyranny, which the men of our choice have conferred on the President, and the President of our choice has assented to and accepted, over the friendly strangers, to whom the mild spirit of our country and its laws had pledged hospitality and protection; that the men of our choice have more respected the bare suspicions of the President than the solid rights of innocence, the claims of justification, the sacred force of truth, and the forms and substance of law and justice.

In questions of power, then, let no more be said of confidence in man, but bind him down from mischief by the chains of the Constitution. That this commonwealth does therefore call on its co-states for an expression of their sentiments on the acts concerning aliens, and for the punishment of certain crimes herein before specified, plainly declaring whether these acts are or are not authorized by the federal compact. And it doubts not that their sense will be so announced as to prove their attachment to limited government, whether general or particular, and that the rights and liberties of their co-states will be exposed to no dangers by remaining embarked on a common bottom with their own; but they will concur with this commonwealth in considering the said acts as so palpably against the Constitution as to amount to an undisguised declaration, that the compact is not meant to be the measure of the powers of the general government, but that it will proceed in the exercise over these states of all powers whatsoever. That they will view this as seizing the rights of the states, and consolidating them in the hands of the general government, with a power assumed to bind the states, not merely in cases made federal, but in all cases whatsoever, by laws made, not with their consent, but by others against their consent; that this would be to surrender the form of government we have chosen, and live under one deriving its powers from its own will, and not from our authority; and that the co-states, recurring to their natural rights not made federal, will concur in declaring these void and of no force, and will each unite with this commonwealth in requesting their repeal at the next session of Congress.

EDMUND BULLOCK, S. H. R.
JOHN CAMPBELL, S. S. P. T.
Passed the House of Representatives, Nov. 10, 1798.
Attest, THO'S. TODD, C. H. R.

In Senate, Nov. 13, 1798—Unanimously concurred in.
Attest, B. THURSTON, C. S.

Approved, November 19, 1798.
By the Governor, JAMES GARRARD, *Governor of Kentucky.*
HARRY TOULMIN, *Secretary of State.*

The Virginia Resolutions of 1798

Pronouncing the Alien and Sedition laws to be unconstitutional, and defining the rights of the States.

Drawn by Mr. Madison.

In the Virginia House of Delegates, Friday, December 21, 1798.

—

Resolved, That the General Assembly of Virginia doth unequivocally express a firm resolution to maintain and defend the Constitution of the United States, and the Constitution of this state, against every aggression, either foreign or domestic; and that they will support the government of the United States in all measures warranted by the former.

That this Assembly most solemnly declares a warm attachment to the union of the states, to maintain which it pledges its powers; and that, for this end, it is their duty to watch over and oppose every infraction of those principles which constitute the only basis of that union, because a faithful observance of them can alone secure its existence and the public happiness.

That this Assembly doth explicitly and peremptorily declare, that it views the powers of the federal government as resulting from the compact to which the states are parties, as limited by the plain sense and intention of the instrument constituting that compact, as no further valid than they are authorized by the grants enumerated in that compact; and that, in case of a deliberate, palpable, and dangerous exercise of other powers, not granted by the said compact, the states, who are parties thereto, have the right, and are in duty bound, to interpose, for arresting the progress of the evil, and for maintaining, within their respective limits, the authorities, rights, and liberties, appertaining to them.

That the General Assembly doth also express its deep regret, that a spirit has, in sundry instances, been manifested by the federal government to enlarge its powers by forced constructions of the constitutional charter which defines them; and that indications have appeared of a design to expound certain general phrases (which, having been copied from the very limited grant of powers in the former Articles of Confederation, were the less liable to be misconstrued) so as to destroy the meaning and effect of the particular enumeration which necessarily explains and limits the general phrases, and so as to consolidate the states, by degrees, into one sovereignty, the obvious tendency and inevitable result of which would be, to transform the present republican system of the United States into an absolute, or, at best, a mixed monarchy.

That the General Assembly doth particularly PROTEST against the palpable and alarming infractions of the Constitution, in the two late cases of the "Alien and Sedition Acts," passed at the last session of Congress; the first of which exercises a power nowhere delegated to the federal government, and which, by uniting legislative and judicial powers to those of executive, subverts the general principles of free government, as well as the particular organization and positive provisions of the Federal Constitution; and the other of which acts exercises, in like manner, a power not delegated by the Constitution, but, on the contrary, expressly and positively forbidden by one of the amendments thereto,—a power which, more than any other, ought to produce universal alarm, because it is levelled against the right of freely examining public characters and measures, and of free communication among the people thereon, which has ever been justly deemed the only effectual guardian of every other right.

That this state having, by its Convention, which ratified the Federal Constitution, expressly declared that, among other essential rights, "the liberty of conscience and the press cannot be cancelled, abridged, restrained, or modified, by any authority of the United States," and from its extreme anxiety to guard these rights from every possible attack of sophistry and ambition, having, with other states, recommended an amendment for that purpose, which amendment was, in due time, annexed to the Constitution,—it would mark a reproachful inconsistency, and criminal degeneracy, if an indifference were now shown to the most palpable violation of one of the rights thus declared and secured, and to the establishment of a precedent which may be fatal to the other.

That the good people of this commonwealth, having ever felt, and continuing to feel, the most sincere affection for their brethren of the other states; the truest anxiety for establishing and perpetuating the union of all; and the most scrupulous fidelity to that Constitution, which is the pledge of mutual friendship, and the instrument of mutual happiness,—the General Assembly doth solemnly appeal to the like dispositions in the other states, in confidence that they will concur with this commonwealth in declaring, as it does hereby declare, that the acts aforesaid are unconstitutional; and that the necessary and proper measures will be taken *by each* for coöperating with this state, in maintaining unimpaired the authorities, rights, and liberties, reserved to the states respectively, or to the people.

That the governor be desired to transmit a copy of the foreging resolutions to the executive authority of each of the other states, with a request that the same may be communicated to the legislature thereof, and that a copy be furnished to each of the senators and representatives representing this state in the Congress of the United States.

Attest, JOHN STEWART.
1798, December 24. Agreed to by the Senate.
H. BROOKE.

A true copy from the original deposited in the office of the General Assembly. JOHN STEWART, *Keeper of Rolls.*

Extracts from the Address to the People, Which Accompanied the Foregoing Resolutions

—

Fellow-citizens: Unwilling to shrink from our representative responsibilities, conscious of the purity of our motives, but acknowledging your right to supervise our conduct, we invite your serious attention to the emergency which dictated the subjoined resolutions. Whilst we disdain to alarm you by ill-founded jealousies, we recommend an investigation guided by the coolness of wisdom, and a decision bottomed on firmness, but tempered with moderation.

It would be perfidious in those intrusted with the GUARDIANSHIP OF THE STATE SOVEREIGNTY, and acting under the solemn obligation of the following oath,—"I do swear that I will support the Constitution of the United States,"—not to warn you of encroachments, which, though clothed with the pretext of necessity, or disguised by arguments of expediency, may yet establish precedents which may ultimately devote a generous and unsuspicious people to all the consequences of usurped power.

Encroachments springing from a government WHOSE ORGANIZATION CANNOT BE MAINTAINED WITHOUT THE CO-OPERATION OF THE STATES, furnish the strongest excitements upon the state legislatures to watchfulness, and impose upon them the strongest obligation TO PRESERVE UNIMPAIRED THE LINE OF PARTITION.

The acquiescence of the states, under infractions of the federal compact, would either beget a speedy consolidation, by precipitating the state governments into impotency and contempt, or prepare the way for a revolution, by a repetition of these infractions until the people are aroused to appear in the majesty of their strength. It is to avoid these calamities that we exhibit to the people the momentous question, whether the Constitution of the United States shall yield to a construction which defies every restraint, and overwhelms the best hopes of republicanism.

Exhortations to disregard domestic usurpation, until foreign danger shall have passed, is an artifice which may be forever used; because the possessors of power, who are the advocates for its extension, can ever create national embarrassments, to be successively employed to soothe the people into sleep, whilst that power is swelling, silently, secretly, and fatally. Of the same character are insinuations of a foreign influence, which seize upon a laudable enthusiasm against danger from abroad, and distort it by an unnatural application, so as to blind your eyes against danger at home.

The Sedition Act presents a scene which was never expected by the early friends of the Constitution. It was then admitted that the state sovereignties were only diminished by powers specifically enumerated, or necessary to carry the specified powers into effect. Now, federal authority is deduced from implication; and from the existence of state law, it is inferred that Congress possess a similar power of legislation; whence Congress will be endowed with a power of legislation in all cases whatsoever, and the states will be stripped of every right reserved, by the concurrent claims of a paramount legislature.

The Sedition Act is the offspring of these tremendous pretensions, which inflict a death-wound on the sovereignty of the states.

For the honor of American understanding, we will not believe that the people have been allured into the adoption of the Constitution by an affectation of defining powers, whilst the *preamble* would admit a construction which would erect the will of Congress into a power paramount in all cases, and therefore limited in none. On the contrary, it is evident that the objects for which the Constitution was formed were deemed attainable only by a particular enumeration and specification of each power granted to the federal government; reserving all others to the people, or to the states. And yet it is in vain we search for any specified power embracing the right of legislation against the freedom of the press.

Had the states been despoiled of their sovereignty by the generality of the preamble, and had the federal government been endowed with whatever they should judge to be instrumental towards the union, justice, tranquillity, common defence, general welfare, and the preservation of liberty, nothing could have been more frivolous than an enumeration of powers.

All the preceding arguments, arising from a deficiency of constitutional power in Congress, apply to the Alien Act; and this act is liable to other objections peculiar to itself. If a suspicion that aliens are dangerous, constitutes the justification of that power exercised over them by Congress, then a similar suspicion will justify the exercise of a similar power over natives; because there is nothing in the Constitution distinguishing between the power of a state to permit the residence of natives and aliens. It is, therefore, a right originally possessed, and never surrendered, by the respective states, and which is rendered dear and valuable to Virginia, because it is assailed through the bosom of the Constitution, and because her peculiar situation renders the easy admission of artisans and laborers an interest of vast importance.

But this bill contains other features, still more alarming and dangerous. It dispenses with the trial by jury; it violates the judicial system; it confounds legislative, executive, and judicial powers; it punishes without trial; and it bestows upon the President despotic power over a numerous class of men. Are such measures consistent with our constitutional principles? And will an accumulation of power so extensive in the hands of the executive, over aliens, secure to natives the blessings of republican liberty?

If measures can mould governments, and if an uncontrolled power of construction is surrendered to those who administer them, their progress may be easily foreseen, and their end easily foretold. A lover of monarchy, who opens the treasures of corruption by distributing emolument among devoted partisans, may at the same time be approaching his object and deluding the people with professions of republicanism. He may confound monarchy and republicanism, by the art of definition. He may varnish over the dexterity which ambition never fails to display, with the pliancy of language, the seduction of expediency, or the prejudices of the times; and he may come at length to avow, that so extensive a territory as that of the United States can only be governed by the energies of monarchy; that it cannot be defended, except by standing armies; and that it cannot be united, except by consolidation.

Measures have already been adopted which may lead to these consequences. They consist—

In fiscal systems and arrangements, which keep a host of commercial and wealthy individuals imbodied, and obedient to the mandates of the treasury;—

In armies and navies, which will, on the one hand, enlist the tendency of man to pay homage to his fellow-creature who can feed or honor him; and on the other, employ the principle of fear, by punishing imaginary insurrections, under the pretext of preventive justice;—

In swarms of officers, civil and military, who can inculcate political tenets tending to consolidation and monarchy, both by indulgences and severities, and can act as spies over the free exercise of human reason;—

In restraining the freedom of the press, and investing the executive with legislative, executive, and judicial powers, over a numerous body of men;—

And, that we may shorten the catalogue, in establishing, by successive precedents, such a mode of construing the Constitution as will rapidly remove every restraint upon federal power.

Let history be consulted; let the man of experience reflect; nay, let the artificers of monarchy be asked what further materials they can need for building up their favorite system.

These are solemn but painful truths; and yet we recommend it to you not to forget the possibility of danger from without, although danger threatens us from within. Usurpation is indeed dreadful; but against foreign invasion, if that should happen, let us rise with hearts and hands united, and repel the attack with the zeal of freemen who will strengthen their title to examine and correct domestic measures, by having defended their country against foreign aggression.

Pledged as we are, fellow-citizens, to these sacred engagements, we yet humbly, fervently implore the Almighty Disposer of events to avert from our land war and usurpation, the scourges of mankind; to permit our fields to be cultivated in peace; to instil into nations the love of friendly intercourse; to suffer our youth to be educated in virtue, and to preserve our morality from the pollution invariably incident to habits of war; to prevent the laborer and husbandman from being harassed by taxes and imposts; to remove from ambition the means of disturbing the commonwealth; to annihilate all pretexts for power afforded by war; to maintain the Constitution; and to bless our nation with tranquillity, under whose benign influence we may reach the summit of happiness and glory, to which we are destined by *nature* and *nature's God.*

Attest, JOHN STEWART, C. H. D.
1799, January 23d. Agreed to by the Senate. H. BROOKE, C.S.

A true copy from the original deposited in the office of the General Assembly. JOHN STEWART, *Keeper of Rolls.*

Answers of the Several State Legislatures

STATE OF DELAWARE.

In the House of Representatives, February 1, 1799.

—

Resolved, By the Senate and House of Representatives of the state of Delaware, in General Assembly met, that they consider the resolutions from the state of Virginia as a very unjustifiable interference with the general government and Constituted authorities of the United States, and of dangerous tendency, and therefore not fit subject for the further consideration of the General Assembly.

ISAAC DAVIS, *Speaker of the Senate.*
STEPHEN LEWIS, *Speaker of the House of Representatives.*
Test, JOHN FISHER, *C. S.*—JOHN CALDWELL, *C. H. R.*

STATE OF RHODE ISLAND AND PROVIDENCE PLANTATIONS.

In General Assembly, February, A. D. 1799.

—

Certain resolutions of the legislature of Virginia, passed on 21st of December last, being communicated to this Assembly,—

1. *Resolved,* That, in the opinion of this legislature, the second section of third article of the Constitution of the United States, in these words, to wit,—"The judicial power shall extend to all cases arising under the laws of the United States,"—vests in the federal courts, exclusively, and in the Supreme Court of the United States, ultimately, the authority of deciding on the constitutionality of any act or law of the Congress of the United States.

2. *Resolved,* That for any state legislature to assume that authority would be—

1st. Blending together legislative and judicial powers;
2d. Hazarding an interruption of the peace of the states by civil discord, in case of a diversity of opinions among the state legislatures; each state having, in that case, no resort, for vindicating its own opinions, but the strength of its own arm;—
3d. Submitting most important questions of law to less competent tribunals; and,
4th. An infraction of the Constitution of the United States, expressed in plain terms.

3. *Resolved,* That, although, for the above reasons, this legislature, in their public capacity, do not feel themselves

authorized to consider and decide on the constitutionality of the Sedition and Alien laws, (so called,) yet they are called upon, by the exigency of this occasion, to declare that, in their private opinions, these laws are within the powers delegated to Congress, and promotive of the welfare of the United States.

4. *Resolved,* That the governor communicate these resolutions to the supreme executive of the state of Virginia, and at the same time express to him that this legislature cannot contemplate, without extreme concern and regret, the many evil and fatal consequences which may flow from the very unwarrantable resolutions aforesaid of the legislature of Virginia, passed on the twenty-first day of December last.

A true copy, SAMUEL EDDY, *Secretary.*

COMMONWEALTH OF MASSACHUSETTS.

In Senate, February 9, 1799.

—

The legislature of Massachusetts, having taken into serious consideration the resolutions of the state of Virginia, passed the 21st day of December last, and communicated by his excellency the governor, relative to certain supposed infractions of the Constitution of the United States, by the government thereof; and being convinced that the Federal Constitution is calculated to promote the happiness, prosperity, and safety, of the people of these United States, and to maintain that union of the several states so essential to the welfare of the whole; and being bound by solemn oath to support and defend that Constitution,—feel it unnecessary to make any professions of their attachment to it, or of their firm determination to support it against every aggression, foreign or domestic.

But they deem it their duty solemnly to declare that, while they hold sacred the principle, that consent of the people is the only pure source of just and legitimate power, they cannot admit the right of the state legislatures to denounce the administration of that government to which the people themselves, by a solemn compact, have exclusively committed their national concerns. That, although a liberal and enlightened vigilance among the people is always to be cherished, yet an unreasonable jealousy of the men of their choice, and a recurrence to measures of extremity upon groundless or trivial pretexts, have a strong tendency to destroy all national liberty at home, and to deprive the United States of the most essential advantages in relations abroad. That this legislature are persuaded that the decision of all cases in law and equity arising under the Constitution of the United States, and the construction of all laws made in pursuance thereof, are exclusively vested by the people in the judicial courts of the United States.

That the people, in that solemn compact which is declared to be the supreme law of the land, have not constituted the state legislatures the judges of the acts or measures of the federal government, but have confided to them the power of proposing such amendments of the Constitution as shall appear to them necessary to the interests, or conformable to the wishes, of the people whom they represent.

That, by this construction of the Constitution, an amicable and dispassionate remedy is pointed out for any evil which experience may prove to exist, and the peace and prosperity of the United States may be preserved without interruption.

But, should the respectable state of Virginia persist in the assumption of the right to declare the acts of the national government unconstitutional, and should she oppose successfully her force and will to those of the nation, the Constitution would be reduced to a mere cipher, to the form and pageantry of authority, without the energy of power; every act of the federal government which thwarted the views or checked the ambitious projects of a particular state, or of its leading and influential members, would be the object of opposition and of remonstrance; while the people, convulsed and confused by the conflict between two hostile jurisdictions, enjoying the protection of neither, would be wearied into a submission to some bold leader, who would establish himself on the ruins of both.

The legislature of Massachusetts, although they do not themselves claim the right, nor admit the authority of any of the state governments, to decide upon the constitutionality of the acts of the federal government, still, lest their silence should be construed into disapprobation, or at best into a doubt as to the constitutionality of the acts referred to by the state of Virginia; and as the General Assembly of Virginia has called for an expression of their sentiments,—do explicitly declare, that they consider the acts of Congress, commonly called "the Alien and Sedition Acts," not only constitutional; but expedient and necessary: That the former act respects a description of persons whose rights were not particularly contemplated in the Constitution of the United States, who are entitled only to a temporary protection while they yield a temporary allegiance—a protection which ought to be withdrawn whenever they become "dangerous to the public safety," or are found guilty of "treasonable machination" against the government: That Congress, having been especially intrusted by the people with the general defence of the nation, had not only the right, but were bound, to protect it against internal as well as external foes: That the United States, at the time of passing the *Act concerning Aliens,* were threatened with actual invasion; had been driven, by the unjust and ambitious conduct of the French government, into warlike preparations, expensive and burdensome; and had then, within the bosom of the country, thousands of aliens, who, we doubt not, were ready to coöperate in an external attack.

It cannot be seriously believed that the United States should have waited till the poniard had in fact been plunged. The removal of aliens is the usual preliminary of hostility, and is justified by the invariable usages of nations. Actual hostility had unhappily long been experienced, and a formal declaration of it the government had reason daily to expect. The law, therefore, was just and salutary; and no officer could with so much propriety be intrusted with the execution of it, as the one in whom the Constitution has reposed the executive power of the United States.

The *Sedition Act,* so called, is, in the opinion of this legislature, equally defensible. The General Assembly of Virginia, in their resolve under consideration, observe, that when that state, by its Convention, ratified the Federal Constitution, it expressly declared, "that, among other essential rights, the liberty of conscience and of the press cannot be cancelled, abridged, restrained, or modified, by any authority of the United States," and, from its extreme anxiety to guard these rights from every possible attack of sophistry or ambition, with other states, recommended an amendment for that purpose; which amendment was, in due time, annexed to the Constitution; but they did not surely expect that the proceedings of their state Convention were to explain the amendment adopted by the Union. The words of that amendment, on this subject, are, "Congress shall make no law abridging the freedom of speech or of the press."

The act complained of is no abridgment of the freedom of either. The genuine liberty of speech and the press is the liberty to utter and publish the truth; but the constitutional right of the citizen to utter and publish the truth is not to be confounded with the licentiousness, in speaking and writing, that is only employed in propagating falsehood and slander. This freedom of the press has been explicitly secured by most, if not all the state constitutions; and of this provision there has been generally but one construction among enlightened men—that it is a security for the rational use, and not the abuse of the press; of which the courts of law, the juries and people will judge: this right is not infringed, but confirmed and established, by the late act of Congress.

By the Constitution, the legislative, executive, and judicial departments of government are ordained and established; and general enumerated powers vested in them respectively, including those which are prohibited to the several states. Certain powers are granted, in general terms, by the people, to their general government, for the purposes of their safety and protection. The government is not only empowered, but it is made their duty, to repel invasions and suppress insurrections; to guaranty to the several states a republican form of government; to protect each state against invasion, and, when applied to, against domestic violence; to hear and decide all cases in law and equity arising under the Constitution, and under any treaty or law made in pursuance thereof; and all cases of admiralty and maritime jurisdiction, and relating to the law of nations. Whenever, therefore, it becomes necessary to effect any of the objects designated, it is perfectly consonant to all just rules of construction to infer that the usual means and powers necessary to the attainment of that object are also granted. But the Constitution has left no occasion to resort to implication for these powers; it has made an express grant of them, in the 8th section of the 1st article, which ordains, "that Congress shall have power to make all laws which shall be necessary and proper for carrying into execution the foregoing powers, and all other powers vested by the Constitution in the government of the United States, or in any department or officer thereof."

This Constitution has established a Supreme Court of the United States, but has made no provision for its protection, even against such improper conduct in its presence, as might disturb its proceedings, unless expressed in the section before recited. But as no statute has been passed on this subject, this protection is, and has been for nine years past, uniformly found in the application of the principles and usages of the common law. The same protection may unquestionably be afforded by a statute passed in virtue of the before-mentioned section, as necessary and proper for carrying into execution the powers vested in that department. A construction of the different parts of the Constitution, perfectly just and fair, will, on analogous principles, extend protection and security, against the offences in question, to the other departments of government, in discharge of their respective trusts.

The President of the United States is bound by his oath "to preserve, protect, and defend, the Constitution;" and it is expressly made his duty "to take care that the laws be faithfully executed." But this would be impracticable by any created being, if there could be no legal restraint of those scandalous misrepresentations of his measures and motives which directly tend to rob him of the public confidence; and equally impotent would be every other public officer, if thus left to the mercy of the seditious.

It is holden to be a truth most clear, that the important trusts before enumerated cannot be discharged by the government to which they are committed, without the power to restrain seditious practices and unlawful combinations against itself, and to protect the officers thereof from abusive misrepresentations. Had the Constitution withheld this power, it would have made the government responsible for the effects, without any control over the causes which naturally produce them, and would have essentially failed of answering the great ends for which the people of the United States declare, in the first clause of that instrument, that they establish the same—viz., "to form a more perfect union, establish justice, insure domestic tranquillity, provide for the common defence, promote the general welfare, and secure the blessings of liberty to ourselves and posterity."

Seditious practices and unlawful combinations against the federal government, or any officer thereof, in the performance of his duty, as well as licentiousness of speech and of the press, were punishable, on the principles of common law, in the courts of the United States, before the act in question was passed. This act, then, is an amelioration of that law in favor of the party accused, as it mitigates the punishment which that authorizes, and admits of any investigation of public men and measures which is regulated by truth. It is not intended to protect men in office, only as they are agents of the people. Its object is to afford legal security to public offices and trusts created for the safety and happiness of the people, and therefore the security derived from it is for the benefit of the people, and is their right.

This construction of the Constitution, and of the existing law of the land, as well as the act complained of, the legislature of Massachusetts most deliberately and firmly believe, results from a just and full view of the several parts of the Constitution; and they consider that act to be wise and necessary, as an audacious and unprincipled spirit of falsehood and abuse had been too long unremittingly exerted for the purpose of perverting public opinion, and threatened to undermine and destroy the whole fabric of government.

The legislature further declare, that in the foregoing sentiments they have expressed the general opinion of their constituents, who have not only acquiesced without complaint in those particular measures of the federal government, but have given their explicit approbation by reëlecting those men who voted for the adoption of them. Nor is it apprehended that the citizens of this state will be accused of supineness, or of an indifference to their constitutional rights; for while, on the one hand, they regard with due vigilance the conduct of the government, on the other, their freedom, safety, and happiness require that they should defend that government and its constitutional measures against the open or insidious attacks of any foe, whether foreign or domestic.

And, lastly, that the legislature of Massachusetts feel a strong conviction, that the several United States are connected by a common interest, which ought to render their union indissoluble; and that this state will always coöperate with its confederate states in rendering that union productive of mutual security, freedom, and happiness.

Sent down for concurrence. SAMUEL PHILLIPS, *President.*
In the House of Representatives, February 13, 1799.
Read and concurred. EDWARD H. ROBBINS, *Speaker.*
A true copy. Attest, JOHN AVERY, *Secretary.*

STATE OF NEW YORK.

In Senate, March 5, 1799.

—

Whereas the people of the United States have established for themselves a free and independent national government: And whereas it is essential to the existence of every government, that it have authority to defend and preserve its constitutional powers inviolate, inasmuch as every infringement thereof tends to its subversion: And whereas the judicial power extends expressly to all cases of law and equity arising under the Constitution and the laws of the United States, whereby the interference of the legislatures of the particular states in those cases is manifestly excluded: And whereas our peace, prosperity, and happiness, eminently depend on the preservation of the Union, in order to which a reasonable confidence in the constituted authorities and chosen representatives of the people is indispensable: And whereas every measure calculated to weaken that confidence has a tendency to destroy the usefulness of our public functionaries, and to excite jealousies equally hostile to rational liberty, and the principles of a good republican government: And whereas the Senate, not perceiving that the rights of the particular states have been violated, nor any unconstitutional powers assumed by the general government, cannot forbear to express the anxiety and regret with which they observe the inflammatory and pernicious sentiments and doctrines which are contained in the resolutions of the legislatures of Virginia and Kentucky—sentiments and doctrines no less repugnant to the Constitution of the United States, and the principles of their union, than destructive to the federal government; and unjust to those whom the people have elected to administer it;—wherefore

Resolved, That while the Senate feel themselves constrained to bear unequivocal testimony against such sentiments and doctrines, they deem it a duty no less indispensable explicitly to declare their incompetency, as a branch of the legislature of this state, to supervise the acts of the general government,

Resolved, That his excellency, the governor, be, and he is hereby, requested to transmit a copy of the foregoing resolution to the executives of the states of Virginia and Kentucky, to the end that the same may be communicated to the legislatures thereof.

A true copy. ABM. B. BAUCKER, *Clerk.*

STATE OF CONNECTICUT.

—

At a General Assembly of the state of Connecticut, holden at Hartford, in the said state, on the second Thursday of May, Anno Domini 1799, his excellency, the governor, having communicated to this Assembly sundry resolutions of the legislature of Virginia, adopted in December, 1798, which relate to the measures of the general government, and the said resolutions having been considered, it is

Resolved, That this Assembly views with deep regret, and explicitly disavows, the principles contained in the aforesaid resolutions and particularly the opposition to the "Alien and Sedition Acts"—acts which the Constitution authorized, which the exigency of the country rendered necessary, which the constituted authorities have enacted, and which merit the entire approbation of this Assembly. They, therefore, decidedly refuse to concur with the legislature of Virginia in promoting any of the objects attempted in the aforesaid resolutions.

And it is further resolved, That his excellency, the governor, be requested to transmit a copy of the foregoing resolution to the governor of Virginia, that it may be communicated to the legislature of that state.

Passed in the House of Representatives unanimously.
Attest, JOHN C. SMITH, *Clerk.*
Concurred, unanimously, in the Upper House.
Teste, SAMUEL WYLLYS, *Secretary.*

STATE OF NEW HAMPSHIRE.

In the House of Representatives, June 14, 1799.

—

The committee to take into consideration the resolutions of the General Assembly of Virginia, dated December 21, 1798; also certain resolutions of the legislature of Kentucky, of the 10th November, 1798, report as follows:—

The legislature of New Hampshire, having taken into consideration certain resolutions of the General Assembly of Virginia, dated December 21, 1798; also certain resolutions of the legislature of Kentucky, of the 10th of November, 1798:—

Resolved, That the legislature of New Hampshire unequivocally express a firm resolution to maintain and defend the Constitution of the United States, and the Constitution of this state, against every aggression, either foreign or domestic, and that they will support the government of the United States in all measures warranted by the former.

That the state legislatures are not the proper tribunals

to determine the constitutionality of the laws of the general government; that the duty of such decision is properly and exclusively confided to the judicial department.

That, if the legislature of New Hampshire, for mere speculative purposes, were to express an opinion on the acts of the general government, commonly called "the Alien and Sedition Bills," that opinion would unreservedly be, that those acts are constitutional, and, in the present critical situation of our country, highly expedient.

That the constitutionality and expediency of the acts aforesaid have been very ably advocated and clearly demonstrated by many citizens of the United States, more especially by the minority of the General Assembly of Virginia. The legislature of New Hampshire, therefore, deem it unnecessary, by any train of arguments, to attempt further illustration of the propositions, the truth of which, it is confidently believed, at this day, is very generally seen and acknowledged.

Which report, being read and considered, was unanimously received and accepted, one hundred and thirty-seven members being present.

Sent up for concurrence. JOHN PRENTICE, *Speaker.*
In Senate, same day, read and concurred unanimously.
AMOS SHEPARD, *President.*
Approved, June 15, 1799. J. T. GILMAN, *Governor.*
A true copy. Attest, JOSEPH PEARSON, *Secretary.*

STATE OF VERMONT.

In the House of Representatives, October 30, A. D. 1799.

—

The house proceeded to take under their consideration the resolutions of the General Assembly of Virginia, relative to certain measures of the general government, transmitted to the legislature of this state, for their consideration: Whereupon,—

Resolved, That the General Assembly of the state of Vermont do highly disapprove of the resolutions of the General Assembly of Virginia, as being unconstitutional in their nature, and dangerous in their tendency. It belongs not to state legislatures to decide on the constitutionality of laws made by the general government; this power being exclusively vested in the judiciary courts of the Union. That his excellency, the governor, be requested to transmit a copy of this resolution to the executive of Virginia, to be communicated to the General Assembly of that state: And that the same be sent to the governor and council for their concurrence.

SAMUEL C. CRAFTS, *Clerk.*

In Council, October 30, 1799. Read and concurred unanimously.

RICHARD WHITNEY, *Secretary.*

The Kentucky Resolutions of 1799

The original draft prepared by Thomas Jefferson.

House of Representatives, Thursday, Nov. 14, 1799.

—

The house, according to the standing order of the day, resolved itself into a committee of the whole house, on the state of the commonwealth, (Mr. Desha in the chair,) and, after some time spent therein, the speaker resumed the chair, and Mr. Desha reported, that the committee had taken under consideration sundry resolutions passed by several state legislatures, on the subject of the Alien and Sedition Laws, and had come to a resolution thereupon, which he delivered in at the clerk's table, where it was read and *unanimously* agreed to by the house, as follows:—

The representatives of the good people of this commonwealth, in General Assembly convened, having maturely considered the answers of sundry states in the Union to their resolutions, passed the last session, respecting certain unconstitutional laws of Congress, commonly called the Alien and Sedition Laws, would be faithless, indeed, to themselves, and to those they represent, were they silently to acquiesce in the principles and doctrines attempted to be maintained in all those answers, that of Virginia only excepted. To again enter the field of argument, and attempt more fully or forcibly to expose the unconstitutionality of those obnoxious laws, would, it is apprehended, be as unnecessary as unavailing. We cannot, however, but lament that, in the discussion of those interesting subjects by sundry of the legislatures of our sister states, unfounded suggestions and uncandid insinuations, derogatory to the true character and principles of this commonwealth, have been substituted in place of fair reasoning and sound argument. Our opinions of these alarming measures of the general government, together with our reasons for those opinions, were detailed with decency and with temper, and submitted to the discussion and judgment of our fellow-citizens throughout the Union. Whether the like decency and temper have been observed in the answers of most of those states who have denied, or attempted to obviate, the great truths contained in those resolutions, we have now only to submit to a candid world. Faithful to the true principles of the federal Union, unconscious of any designs to disturb the harmony of that Union, and anxious only to escape the fangs of despotism, the good people of this commonwealth are regardless of censure or calumniation. Lest, however, the silence of this commonwealth should be construed into an acquiescence in the doctrines and principles advanced, and attempted to be maintained, by the said answers; or at least those of our fellow-citizens, throughout the Union, who so widely differ from us on those important subjects, should be deluded by the expectation that we shall be deterred from what we conceive our duty, or shrink from the principles contained in those resolutions,—therefore,

Resolved, That this commonwealth considers the federal Union, upon the terms and for the purposes specified in the late compact, conducive to the liberty and happiness of the several states: That it does now unequivocally declare its attachment to the Union, and to that compact, agreeably to its obvious and real intention, and will be among the last to seek its dissolution: That, if those who administer the general government be permitted to transgress the limits fixed by that compact, by a total disregard to the special delegations of power therein contained, an annihilation of the state governments, and the creation, upon their ruins, of a general consolidated government, will be the inevitable consequence: That the principle and construction, contended for by sundry of the state legislatures, that the general government is the exclusive judge of the extent of the powers delegated to it, stop not short of *despotism*—since the discretion of those who administer the government, and not the *Constitution,* would be the measure of their powers: That the several states who formed that instrument, being sovereign and independent, have the unquestionable right to judge of the infraction; and, *That a nullification, by those sovereignties, of all unauthorized acts done under color of that instrument, is the rightful remedy:* That this commonwealth does, under the most deliberate reconsideration, declare, that the said Alien and Sedition Laws are, in their opinion, palpable violations of the said Constitution; and, however cheerfully it may be disposed to surrender its opinion to a majority of its sister states, in matters of ordinary or doubtful policy, yet, in momentous regulations like the present, which so vitally wound the best rights of the citizen, it would consider a silent acquiescence as highly criminal: That, although this commonwealth, as a party to the federal compact, will bow to the laws of the Union, yet it does, at the same time, declare, that it will not now, or ever hereafter, cease to oppose, in a constitutional manner, every attempt, at what quarter soever offered, to violate that compact: And finally, in order that no pretext or arguments may be drawn from a supposed acquiescence, on the part of this commonwealth, in the constitutionality of those laws, and be thereby used as precedents for similar future violations of the federal compact, this commonwealth does now enter against them its solemn PROTEST.

Extract, &c. Attest, THOMAS TODD, *C. H. R.*
In Senate, Nov. 22, 1799.—Read and concurred in.
Attest, B. THURSTON, *C. S.*

Report on the Virginia Resolutions

James Madison

House of Delegates, Session of 1799–1800.

Report of the Committee to whom were referred the Communications of various States, relative to the Resolutions of the last General Assembly of this State, concerning the Alien and Sedition Laws.

Whatever room might be found in the proceedings of some of the states, who have disapproved of the resolutions of the General Assembly of this commonwealth, passed on the 21st day of December, 1798, for painful remarks on the spirit and manner of those proceedings, it appears to the committee most consistent with the duty, as well as dignity, of the General Assembly, to hasten an oblivion of every circumstance which might be construed into a diminution of mutual respect, confidence, and affection, among the members of the Union.

The committee have deemed it a more useful task to revise, with a critical eye, the resolutions which have met with their disapprobation; to examine fully the several objections and arguments which have appeared against them; and to inquire whether there can be any errors of fact, of principle, or of reasoning, which the candor of the General Assembly ought to acknowledge and correct.

The *first* of the resolutions is in the words following:—

> "*Resolved,* That the General Assembly of Virginia doth unequivocally express a firm resolution to maintain and defend the Constitution of the United States, and the Constitution of this state, against every aggression, either foreign or domestic; and that they will support the government of the United States in all measures warranted by the former."

No unfavorable comment can have been made on the sentiments here expressed. To maintain and defend the Constitution of the United States, and of their own state, against every aggression, both foreign and domestic, and to support the government of the United States in all measures warranted by their Constitution, are duties which the General Assembly ought always to feel, and to which, on such an occasion, it was evidently proper to express their sincere and firm adherence.

In their *next* resolution—

> "That General Assembly most solemnly declares a warm attachment to the union of the states, to maintain which it pledges all its powers; and that, for this end, it is their duty to watch over and oppose every infraction of those principles which constitute the only basis of that Union, because a faithful observance of them can alone secure its existence and the public happiness."

The observation just made is equally applicable to this solemn declaration of warm attachment to the Union, and this solemn pledge to maintain it; nor can any question arise among enlightened friends of the Union, as to the duty of watching over and opposing every infraction of those principles which constitute its basis, and a faithful observance of which can alone secure its existence, and the public happiness thereon depending.

The *third* resolution is in the words following:—

> "That this Assembly doth explicitly and peremptorily declare, that it views the powers of the federal government, as resulting from the compact to which the states are parties, as limited by the plain sense and intention of the instrument constituting that compact—as no further valid than they are authorized by the grants enumerated in that compact; and that, in case of a deliberate, palpable, and dangerous exercise of other powers, not granted by the said compact, the states who are parties thereto have the right, and are in duty bound, to interpose, for arresting the progress of the evil, and for main-

taining, within their respective limits, the authorities, rights, and liberties, appertaining to them."

On this resolution the committee have bestowed all the attention which its importance merits. They have *scanned* it not merely with a strict, but with a severe eye; and they feel confidence in pronouncing that, in its just and fair construction, it is unexceptionably true in its several positions, as well as constitutional and conclusive in its inferences.

The resolution declares, *first,* that "it views the powers of the federal government as resulting from the compact to which the states are parties;" in other words, that the federal powers are derived from the Constitution; and that the Constitution is a compact to which the states are parties.

Clear as the position must seem, that the federal powers are derived from the Constitution, and from that alone, the committee are not unapprized of a late doctrine which opens another source of federal powers, not less extensive and important than it is new and unexpected. The examination of this doctrine will be most conveniently connected with a review of a succeeding resolution. The committee satisfy themselves here with briefly remarking that, in all the contemporary discussions and comments which the Constitution underwent, it was constantly justified and recommended on the ground that the powers not given to the government were withheld from it; and that, if any doubt could have existed on this subject, under the original text of the Constitution, it is removed, as far as words could remove it, by the 12th amendment, now a part of the Constitution, which expressly declares, "that the powers not delegated to the United States by the Constitution, nor prohibited by it to the states, are reserved to the states respectively, or to the people."

The other position involved in this branch of the resolution, namely, "that the states are parties to the Constitution," or compact, is, in the judgment of the committee, equally free from objection. It is indeed true that the term "states" is sometimes used in a vague sense, and sometimes in different senses, according to the subject to which it is applied. Thus it sometimes means the separate sections of territory occupied by the political societies within each; sometimes the particular governments established by those societies; sometimes those societies as organized into those particular governments; and lastly, it means the people composing those political societies, in their highest sovereign capacity. Although it might be wished that the perfection of language admitted less diversity in the signification of the same words, yet little inconvenience is produced by it, where the true sense can be collected with certainty from the different applications. In the present instance, whatever different construction of the term "states," in the resolution, may have been entertained, all will at least concur in that last mentioned; because in that sense the Constitution was submitted to the "states;" in that sense the "states" ratified it; and in that sense of the term "states," they are consequently parties to the compact from which the powers of the federal government result.

The next position is, that the General Assembly views the powers of the federal government "as limited by the plain sense and intention of the instrument constituting that compact," and "as no further valid than they are authorized by the grants therein enumerated." It does not seem possible that any just objection can lie against either of these clauses. The first amounts merely to a declaration that the compact ought to have the interpretation plainly intended by the parties to it; the other, to a declaration that it ought to have the execution and effect intended by them. If the powers granted be valid, it is solely because they are granted; and if the granted powers are valid because granted, all other powers not granted must not be valid.

The resolution, having taken this view of the federal compact, proceeds to infer, "That, in case of a deliberate, palpable, and dangerous exercise of other powers, not granted by the said compact, the states, who are parties thereto, have the right, and are in duty bound, to interpose for arresting the progress of the evil, and for maintaining, within their respective limits, the authorities, rights, and liberties, appertaining to them."

It appears to your committee to be a plain principle, founded in common sense, illustrated by common practice, and essential to the nature of compacts, that, where resort can be had to no tribunal superior to the authority of the parties, the parties themselves must be the rightful judges, in the last resort, whether the bargain made has been pursued or violated. The Constitution of the United States was formed by the sanction of the states, given by each in its sovereign capacity. It adds to the stability and dignity, as well as to the authority, of the Constitution, that it rests on this legitimate and solid foundation. The states, then, being the parties to the constitutional compact, and in their sovereign capacity, it follows of necessity that there can be no tribunal, above their authority, to decide, in the last resort, whether the compact made by them be violated;

and consequently, that, as the parties to it, they must themselves decide, in the last resort, such questions as may be of sufficient magnitude to require their interposition.

It does not follow, however, because the states, as sovereign parties to their constitutional compact, must ultimately decide whether it has been violated, that such a decision ought to be interposed either in a hasty manner or on doubtful and inferior occasions. Even in the case of ordinary conventions between different nations, where, by the strict rule of interpretation, a breach of a part may be deemed a breach of the whole,—every part being deemed a condition of every other part, and of the whole,—it is always laid down that the breach must be both wilful and material, to justify an application of the rule. But in the case of an intimate and constitutional union, like that of the United States, it is evident that the interposition of the parties, in their sovereign capacity, can be called for by occasions only deeply and essentially affecting the vital principles of their political system.

The resolution has, accordingly, guarded against any misapprehension of its object, by expressly requiring, for such an interposition, "the case of a deliberate, palpable, and dangerous breach of the Constitution, by the exercise of powers not granted by it." It must be a case not of a light and transient nature, but of a nature dangerous to the great purposes for which the Constitution was established. It must be a case, moreover, not obscure or doubtful in its construction, but plain and palpable. Lastly, it must be a case not resulting from a partial consideration or hasty determination, but a case stamped with a final consideration and deliberate adherence. It is not necessary, because the resolution does not require, that the question should be discussed, how far the exercise of any particular power, ungranted by the Constitution, would justify the interposition of the parties to it. As cases might easily be stated, which none would contend ought to fall within that description,—cases, on the other hand, might, with equal ease, be stated, so flagrant and so fatal as to unite every opinion in placing them within the description.

But the resolution has done more than guard against misconstruction, by expressly referring to cases of a deliberate, palpable, and dangerous nature. It specifies the object of the interposition, which it contemplates, to be solely that of arresting the progress of the evil of usurpation, and of maintaining the authorities, rights, and liberties, appertaining to the states, as parties to the Constitution.

From this view of the resolution, it would seem inconceivable that it can incur any just disapprobation from those who, laying aside all momentary impressions, and recollecting the genuine source and object of the Federal Constitution, shall candidly and accurately interpret the meaning of the General Assembly. If the deliberate exercise of dangerous powers, palpably withheld by the Constitution, could not justify the parties to it in interposing even so far as to arrest the progress of the evil, and thereby to preserve the Constitution itself, as well as to provide for the safety of the parties to it, there would be an end to all relief from usurped power, and a direct subversion of the rights specified or recognized under all the state constitutions, as well as a plain denial of the fundamental principle on which our independence itself was declared.

But it is objected, that the judicial authority is to be regarded as the sole expositor of the Constitution in the last resort; and it may be asked for what reason the declaration by the General Assembly, supposing it to be theoretically true, could be required at the present day, and in so solemn a manner.

On this objection it might be observed, first, that there may be instances of usurped power, which the forms of the Constitution would never draw within the control of the judicial department; secondly, that, if the decision of the judiciary be raised above the authority of the sovereign parties to the Constitution, the decisions of the other departments, not carried by the forms of the Constitution before the judiciary, must be equally authoritative and final with the decisions of that department. But the proper answer to the objection is, that the resolution of the General Assembly relates to those great and extraordinary cases, in which all the forms of the Constitution may prove ineffectual against infractions dangerous to the essential rights of the parties to it. The resolution supposes that dangerous powers, not delegated, may not only be usurped and executed by the other departments, but that the judicial department, also, may exercise or sanction dangerous powers beyond the grant of the Constitution; and, consequently, that the ultimate right of the parties to the Constitution, to judge whether the compact has been dangerously violated, must extend to violations by one delegated authority as well as by another—by the judiciary as well as by the executive, or the legislature.

However true, therefore, it may be, that the judicial department is, in all questions submitted to it by the forms of the Constitution, to decide in the last resort, this resort must necessarily be deemed the last in relation to the authorities of the other departments of the government; not in relation to the rights of the parties to the constitutional compact, from which the judicial, as well as the other departments, hold their delegated trusts. On any other hypothesis, the delegation of judicial power would annul the authority delegating it; and the concurrence of this department with the others in usurped powers, might subvert forever, and beyond the possible reach of any rightful remedy, the very Constitution which all were instituted to preserve.

The truth declared in the resolution being established, the expediency of making the declaration at the present day may safely be left to the temperate consideration and candid judgment of the American public. It will be remembered, that a frequent recurrence to fundamental principles is solemnly enjoined by most of the state constitutions, and particularly by our own, as a necessary safeguard against the danger of degeneracy, to which republics are liable, as well as other governments, though in a less degree than others. And a fair comparison of the political doctrines not unfrequent at the present day, with those which characterized the epoch of our revolution, and which form the basis of our republican constitutions, will best determine whether the declaratory recurrence here made to those principles ought to be viewed as unseasonable and improper, or as a vigilant discharge of an important duty. The authority of constitutions over governments, and of the sovereignty of the people over constitutions, are truths which are at all times necessary to be kept in mind; and at no time, perhaps, more necessary than at present.

The fourth resolution stands as follows:—

> "That the General Assembly doth also express its deep regret, that a spirit has, in sundry instances, been manifested by the federal government, to enlarge its powers by forced constructions of the constitutional charter which defines them; and that indications have appeared of a design to expound certain general phrases (which having been copied from the very limited grant of powers in the former Articles of Confederation, were the less liable to be misconstrued) so as to destroy the meaning and effect of the particular enumeration which necessarily explains and limits the general phrases, and so as to consolidate the states, by degrees, into one sovereignty, the obvious tendency and inevitable result of which would be to transform the present republican system of the United States into an absolute, or at best a mixed monarchy."

The *first* question here to be considered is, whether a spirit has, in sundry instances, been manifested by the federal government to enlarge its powers by forced constructions of the constitutional charter.

The General Assembly having declared their opinion, merely, by regretting, in general terms, that forced constructions for enlarging the federal powers have taken place, it does not appear to the committee necessary to go into a specification of every instance to which the resolution may allude. The Alien and Sedition Acts, being particularly named in a succeeding resolution, are of course to be understood as included in the allusion. Omitting others which have less occupied public attention, or been less extensively regarded as unconstitutional, the resolution may be presumed to refer particularly to the bank law, which, from the circumstances of its passage, as well as the latitude of construction on which it is founded, strikes the attention with singular force, and the carriage tax, distinguished also by circumstances in its history having a similar tendency. Those instances alone, if resulting from forced construction, and calculated to enlarge the powers of the federal government,—as the committee cannot but conceive to be the case,—sufficiently warrant this part of the resolution. The committee have not thought it incumbent on them to extend their attention to laws which have been objected to rather as varying the constitutional distribution of powers in the federal government, than as an absolute enlargement of them; because instances of this sort, however important in their principles and tendencies, do not appear to fall strictly within the text under view.

The other questions presenting themselves are, 1. Whether indications have appeared of a design to expound certain general phrases, copied from the "Articles of Confederation," so as to destroy the effect of the particular enumeration explaining and limiting their meaning; 2. Whether this exposition would, by degrees, consolidate the states into one sovereignty; 3. Whether the tendency and result of this consolidation would be to transform the republican system of the United States into a monarchy.

1. The general phrases here meant must be those "of providing for the common defence and general welfare."

In the "Articles of Confederation," the phrases are used as follows, in Art. VIII.: "All charges of war, and all other expenses that shall be incurred for the common defence and general welfare, and allowed by the United States in

Congress assembled, shall be defrayed out of a common treasury, which shall be supplied by the several states, in proportion to the value of all land within each state, granted to or surveyed for any person, as such land, and the buildings and improvements thereon, shall be estimated, according to such mode as the United States in Congress assembled shall, from time to time, direct and appoint."

In the existing Constitution, they make the following part of sect. 8: "The Congress shall have power to lay and collect taxes, duties, imposts, and excises; to pay the debts, and provide for the common defence and general welfare, of the United States."

This similarity in the use of these phrases, in the two great federal charters, might well be considered as rendering their meaning less liable to be misconstrued in the latter; because it will scarcely be said, that in the former they were ever understood to be either a general grant of power, or to authorize the requisition or application of money, by the old Congress, to the common defence and general welfare, except in cases afterwards enumerated, which explained and limited their meaning; and if such was the limited meaning attached to these phrases in the very instrument revised and remodelled by the present Constitution, it can never be supposed that, when copied into this Constitution, a different meaning ought to be attached to them.

That, notwithstanding this remarkable security against misconstruction, a design has been indicated to expound these phrases, in the Constitution, so as to destroy the effect of the particular enumeration of powers by which it explains and limits them, must have fallen under the observation of those who have attended to the course of public transactions. Not to multiply proofs on this subject, it will suffice to refer to the debates of the federal legislature, in which arguments have, on different occasions, been drawn, with apparent effect, from these phrases, in their indefinite meaning.

To these indications might be added, without looking farther, the official report on manufacutures by the late secretary of the treasury, made on the 5th of December, 1791, and the report of a committee of Congress, in January, 1797, on the promotion of agriculture. In the first of these it is expressly contended to belong "to the discretion of the national legislature to pronounce upon the objects which concern the general welfare, and for which, under that description, an appropriation of money is requisite and proper. And there seems to be no room for a doubt, that whatever concerns the general interests of learning, of agriculture, of manufactures, and of commerce, is within the sphere of national councils as far as regards an application of money." The latter report assumes the same latitude of power in the national councils, and applies it to the encouragement of agriculture, by means of a society to be established at the seat of government. Although neither of these reports may have received the sanction of a law carrying it into effect, yet, on the other hand, the extraordinary doctrine contained in both has passed without the slightest positive mark of disapprobation from the authority to which it was addressed.

Now, whether the phrases in question be construed to authorize every measure relating to the common defence and general welfare, as contended by some, or every measure only in which there might be an application of money, as suggested by the caution of others,—the effect must substantially be the same, in destroying the import and force of the particular enumeration of powers which follows these general phrases in the Constitution; for it is evident that there is not a single power whatever which may not have some reference to the common defence or the general welfare; nor a power of any magnitude which, in its exercise, does not involve, or admit, an application of money. The government, therefore, which possesses power in either one or other of these extents, is a government without the limitations formed by a particular enumeration of powers; and, consequently, the meaning and effect of this particular enumeration is destroyed by the exposition given to these general phrases.

This conclusion will not be affected by an attempt to qualify the power over the "general welfare," by referring it to cases where the general welfare is beyond the reach of the separate provisions by the individual states, and leaving to these their jurisdiction in cases to which their separate provisions may be competent; for, as the authority of the individual states must in all cases be incompetent to general regulations operating through the whole, the authority of the United States would be extended to every object relating to the general welfare, which might, by any possibility, be provided for by the general authority. This qualifying construction, therefore, would have little, if any, tendency to circumscribe the power claimed under the latitude of the term "general welfare."

The true and fair construction of this expression, both in the original and existing federal compacts, appears to the committee too obvious to be mistaken. In both, the Congress is authorized to provide money for the common defence and general welfare. In both is subjoined to this authority an enumeration of the cases to which their powers shall extend. Money cannot be applied to the general welfare, otherwise than by an application of it to some particular measure, conducive to the general welfare. Whenever, therefore, money has been raised by the general authority, and is to be applied to a particular measure, a question arises whether the particular measure be within the enumerated authorities vested in Congress. If it be, the money requisite for it may be applied to it. If it be not, no such application can be made. This fair and obvious interpretation coincides with, and is enforced by, the clause in the Constitution which declares that "no money shall be drawn from the treasury but in consequence of appropriations made by law." An appropriation of money to the general welfare would be deemed rather a mockery than an observance of this constitutional injunction.

2. Whether the exposition of the general phrases here combated would not, by degrees, consolidate the states into one sovereignty, is a question concerning which the committee can perceive little room for difference of opinion. To consolidate the states into one sovereignty, nothing more can be wanted than to supersede their respective sovereignties, in the cases reserved to them, by extending the sovereignty of the United States to all cases of the "general welfare"—that is to say, to all cases whatever.

3. That the obvious tendency, and inevitable result, of a consolidation of the states into one sovereignty, would be to transform the republican system of the United States

into a monarchy, is a point which seems to have been sufficiently decided by the general sentiment of America. In almost every instance of discussion relating to the consolidation in question, its certain tendency to pave the way to monarchy seems not to have been contested. The prospect of such a consolidation has formed the only topic of controversy. It would be unnecessary, therefore, for the committee to dwell long on the reasons which support the position of the General Assembly. It may not be improper, however, to remark two consequences, evidently flowing from an extension of the federal power to every subject falling within the idea of the "general welfare."

One consequence must be, to enlarge the sphere of discretion allotted to the executive magistrate. Even within the legislative limits properly defined by the Constitution, the difficulty of accommodating legal regulations to a country so great in extent, and so various in its circumstances, had been much felt, and has led to occasional investments of power in the executive, which involve perhaps as large a portion of discretion as can be deemed consistent with the nature of the executive trust. In proportion as the objects of legislative care might be multiplied, would the time allowed for each be diminished, and the difficulty of providing uniform and particular regulations for all be increased. From these sources would necessarily ensue a greater latitude to the agency of that department which is always in existence, and which could best mould regulations of a general nature, so as to suit them to the diversity of particular situations. And it is in this latitude, as a supplement to the deficiency of the laws, that the degree of executive prerogative materially consists.

The other consequence would be, that of an excessive augmentation of the offices, honors, and emoluments, depending on the executive will. Add to the present legitimate stock all those, of every description, which a consolidation of the states would take from them, and turn over to the federal government, and the patronage of the executive would necessarily be as much swelled, in this case, as its prerogative would be in the other.

This disproportionate increase of prerogative and patronage must evidently either enable the chief magistrate of the Union, by quiet means, to secure his reëlection from time to time, and finally to regulate the succession as he might please; or, by giving so transcendent an importance to the office, would render the election to it so violent and corrupt, that the public voice itself might call for an hereditary in place of an elective succession. Whichever of these events might follow, the transformation of the republican system of the United States into a monarchy, anticipated by the General Assembly from a consolidation of the states into one sovereignty, would be equally accomplished; and whether it would be into a mixed or an absolute monarchy, might depend on too many contingencies to admit of any certain foresight.

The resolution next in order is contained in the following terms:—

> "That the General Assembly doth particularly protest against the palpable and alarming infractions of the Constitution, in the two late cases of the 'Alien and Sedition Acts,' passed at the last session of Congress; the first of which exercises a power nowhere delegated to

the federal government; and which, by uniting legislative and judicial powers to those of the executive, subverts the general principles of free government, as well as the particular organization and positive provisions of the Federal Constitution; and the other of which acts exercises, in like manner, a power not delegated by the Constitution, but, on the contrary, expressly and positively forbidden by one of the amendments thereto—a power which, more than any other, ought to produce universal alarm, because it is levelled against the right of freely examining public characters and measures, and of free communication among the people thereon, which has ever been justly deemed the only effectual guardian of every other right."

The subject of this resolution having, it is presumed, more particularly led the General Assembly into the proceedings which they communicated to the other states, and being in itself of peculiar importance, it deserves the most critical and faithful investigation; for the length of which no apology will be necessary.

The subject divides itself into,—

First, the "Alien Act."

Secondly, the "Sedition Act."

Of the "Alien Act," it is affirmed by the resolution—1. That it exercises a power nowhere delegated to the federal government; 2. That it unites legislative and judicial powers to those of the executive; 3. That this union of powers subverts the general principles of free government; 4. That it subverts the particular organization and positive provisions of the Federal Constitution.

In order to clear the way for a correct view of the first position, several observations will be premised.

In the first place, it is to be borne in mind, that, it being a characteristic feature of the Federal Constitution, as it was originally ratified, and an amendment thereto having precisely declared, "that the powers not delegated to the United States by the Constitution, nor prohibited by it to the states, are reserved to the states respectively, or to the people," it is incumbent in this, as in every other exercise of power by the federal government, to prove, from the Constitution, that it grants the particular power exercised.

The next observation to be made is, that much confusion and fallacy have been thrown into the question, by blending the two cases of *aliens, members of a hostile nation; and aliens, members of friendly nations.* These two cases are so obviously and so essentially distinct, that it occasions no little surprise that the distinction should have been disregarded; and the surprise is so much the greater, as it appears that the two cases are actually distinguished by two separate acts of Congress, passed at the same session, and comprised in the same publication; the one providing for the case of "alien enemies;" the other "concerning aliens" indiscriminately, and consequently extending to aliens of every nation in peace and amity with the United States. With respect to alien enemies, no doubt has been intimated as to the federal authority over them; the Constitution having expressly delegated to Congress the power to declare war against any nation, and of course to treat it and all its members as enemies. With respect to aliens who are not enemies, but members of nations in peace and amity with the United States, the power assumed by the act of

Congress is denied to be constitutional; and it is accordingly against this act that the protest of the General Assembly is expressly and exclusively directed.

A third observation is that, were it admitted, as is contended, that the "act concerning aliens" has for its object, not a *penal,* but a *preventive* justice, it would still remain to be proved that it comes within the constitutional power of the federal legislature; and, if within its power, that the legislature has exercised it in a constitutional manner.

In the administration of preventive justice, the following principles have been held sacred: that some probable ground of suspicion be exhibited before some judicial authority; that it be supported by oath or affirmation; that the party may avoid being thrown into confinement, by finding pledges or sureties for his legal conduct sufficient in the judgment of some judicial authority; that he may have the benefit of a writ of *habeas corpus,* and thus obtain his release if wrongfully confined; and that he may at any time be discharged from his recognizance, or his confinement, and restored to his former liberty and rights, on the order of the proper judicial authority, if it shall see sufficient cause.

All these principles of the only preventive justice known to American jurisprudence are violated by the Alien Act. The ground of suspicion is to be judged of, not by any judicial authority, but by the executive magistrate alone. No oath or affirmation is required. If the suspicion be held reasonable by the President, he may order the suspected alien to depart from the territory of the United States, without the opportunity of avoiding the sentence by finding pledges for his future good conduct. As the President may limit the time of departure as he pleases, the benefit of the writ of *habeas corpus* may be suspended with respect to the party, although the Constitution ordains that it shall not be suspended unless when the public safety may require it, in case of rebellion or invasion,—neither of which existed at the passage of the act; and the party being, under the sentence of the President, either removed from the United States, or being punished by imprisonment, or disqualification ever to become a citizen, on conviction of not obeying the order of removal, he cannot be discharged from the proceedings against him, and restored to the benefits of his former situation, although the *highest judicial authority* should see the most sufficient cause for it.

But, in the last place, it can never be admitted that the removal of aliens, authorized by the act, is to be considered, not as punishment for an offence, but as a measure of precaution and prevention. If the banishment of an alien from a country into which he has been invited as the asylum most auspicious to his happiness,—a country where he may have formed the most tender connections; where he may have invested his entire property, and acquired property of the real and permanent, as well as the movable and temporary kind; where he enjoys, under the laws, a greater share of the blessings of personal security, and personal liberty, than he can elsewhere hope for; and where he may have nearly completed his probationary title to citizenship; if, moreover, in the execution of the sentence against him, he is to be exposed, not only to the ordinary dangers of the sea, but to the peculiar casualties incident to a crisis of war and of unusual licentiousness on that element, and possibly to vindictive purposes, which his emigration itself may have provoked;—if a banishment of this sort be not a punishment, and among the severest of punishments, it will be difficult to imagine a doom to which the name can be applied. And if it be a punishment, it will remain to be inquired, whether it can be constitutionally inflicted, on mere suspicion, by the single will of the executive magistrate, on persons convicted of no personal offence against the laws of the land, nor involved in any offence against the law of nations, charged on the foreign state of which they are members.

One argument offered in justification of this power exercised over aliens is, that, the admission of them into the country being of favor, not of right, the favor is at all times revocable.

To this argument it might be answered, that, allowing the truth of the inference, it would be no proof of what is required. A question would still occur, whether the Constitution had vested the discretionary power of admitting aliens in the federal government or in the state governments.

But it cannot be a true inference, that, because the admission of an alien is a favor, the favor may be revoked at pleasure. A grant of land to an individual may be of favor, not of right; but the moment the grant is made, the favor becomes a right, and must be forfeited before it can be taken away. To pardon a malefactor may be a favor, but the pardon is not, on that account, the less irrevocable. To admit an alien to naturalization, is as much a favor as to admit him to reside in the country; yet it cannot be pretended that a person naturalized can be deprived of the benefits, any more than a native citizen can be disfranchised.

Again, it is said that, aliens not being parties to the Constitution, the rights and privileges which it secures cannot be at all claimed by them.

To this reasoning, also, it might be answered that, although aliens are not parties to the Constitution, it does not follow that the Constitution has vested in Congress an absolute power over them. The parties to the Constitution may have granted, or retained, or modified, the power over aliens, without regard to that particular consideration.

But a more direct reply is, that it does not follow, because aliens are not parties to the Constitution, as citizens are parties to it, that, whilst they actually conform to it, they have no right to its protection. Aliens are not more parties to the laws than they are parties to the Constitution; yet it will not be disputed that, as they owe, on one hand, a temporary obedience, they are entitled, in return, to their protection and advantage.

If aliens had no rights under the Constitution, they might not only be banished, but even capitally punished, without a jury or the other incidents to a fair trial. But so far has a contrary principle been carried, in every part of the United States, that, except on charges of treason, an alien has, besides all the common privileges, the special one of being tried by a jury, of which one half may be also aliens.

It is said, further, that, by the law and practice of nations, aliens may be removed, at discretion, for offences against the law of nations; that Congress are authorized to define and punish such offences; and that to be dangerous to the peace of society is, in aliens, one of those offences.

The distinction between alien enemies and alien friends

is a clear and conclusive answer to this argument. Alien enemies are under the law of nations, and liable to be punished for offences against it. Alien friends, except in the single case of public ministers, are under the municipal law, and must be tried and punished according to that law only.

This argument also, by referring the alien act to the power of Congress to define and *punish* offences against the law of nations, yields the point that the act is of a *penal*, not merely of a preventive operation. It must, in truth, be so considered. And if it be a penal act, the punishment it inflicts must be justified by some offence that deserves it.

Offences for which aliens, within the jurisdiction of a country, are punishable, are—first, offences committed by the nation of which they make a part, and in whose offences they are involved; secondly, offences committed by themselves alone, without any charge against the nation to which they belong. The first is the case of alien enemies; the second, the case of alien friends. In the first case, the offending nation can no otherwise be punished than by war, one of the laws of which authorizes the expulsion of such of its members as may be found within the country against which the offence has been committed. In the second case,—the offence being committed by the individual, not by his nation, and against the municipal law, not against the law of nations,—the individual only, and not the nation, is punishable; and the punishment must be conducted according to the municipal law, not according to the law of nations. Under this view of the subject, the act of Congress for the removal of alien enemies, being conformable to the law of nations, is justified by the Constitution; and the "act" for the removal of alien friends, being repugnant to the constitutional principles of municipal law, is unjustifiable.

Nor is the act of Congress for the removal of alien friends more agreeable to the general practice of nations than it is within the purview of the law of nations. The general practice of nations distinguishes between alien friends and alien enemies. The latter it has proceeded against, according to the law of nations, by expelling them as enemies. The former it has considered as under a local and temporary allegiance, and entitled to a correspondent protection. If contrary instances are to be found in barbarous countries, under undefined prerogatives, or amid revolutionary dangers, they will not be deemed fit precedents for the government of the United States, even if not beyond its constitutional authority.

It is said that Congress may grant letters of marque and reprisal; that reprisals may be made on persons as well as property; and that the removal of aliens may be considered as the exercise, in an inferior degree, of the general power of reprisal on persons.

Without entering minutely into a question that does not seem to require it, it may be remarked that reprisal is a seizure of foreign persons or property, with a view to obtain that justice for injuries done by one state, or its members, to another state, or its members, for which a refusal of the aggressors requires such a resort to force, under the law of nations. It must be considered as an abuse of words, to call the removal of persons from a country a seizure, or a reprisal on them; nor is the distinction to be overlooked between reprisals on persons within the country, and under the faith of its laws, and on persons out of the country. But, laying aside these considerations, it is evidently impossible to bring the alien act within the power of granting reprisals; since it does not allege or imply any injury received from any particular nation, for which this proceeding against its members was intended as a reparation.

The proceeding is authorized against aliens *of every nation;* of nations charged neither with any similar proceedings against American citizens, nor with any injuries for which justice might be sought, in the mode prescribed by the act. Were it true, therefore, that good causes existed for reprisals against one or more foreign nations, and that neither the persons nor property of its members, under the faith of our laws, could plead an exemption, the operation of the act ought to have been limited to the aliens among us belonging to such nations. To license reprisals against all nations, for aggressions charged on one only, would be a measure as contrary to every principle of justice and public law, as to a wise policy, and the universal practice of nations.

It is said that the right of removing aliens is an incident to the power of war, vested in Congress by the Constitution.

This is a former argument in a new shape only, and is answered by repeating, that the removal of alien enemies is an incident to the power of war; that the removal of alien friends is not an incident to the power of war.

It is said that Congress are, by the Constitution, to protect each state against invasion; and that the means of *preventing* invasion are included in the power of protection against it.

The power of war, in general, having been before

granted by the Constitution, this clause must either be a mere specification for greater caution and certainty, of which there are other examples in the instrument, or be the injunction of a duty, superadded to a grant of the power. Under either explanation, it cannot enlarge the powers of Congress on the subject. The power and the duty to protect each state against an invading enemy would be the same under the general power, if this regard to the greater caution had been omitted.

Invasion is an operation of war. To protect against invasion is an exercise of the power of war. A power, therefore, not incident to war, cannot be incident to a particular modification of war; and as the removal of alien friends has appeared to be no incident to a general state of war, it cannot be incident to a partial state, or a particular modification of war.

Nor can it ever be granted, that a power to act on a case, when it actually occurs, includes a power over all the means that may *tend to prevent* the occurrence of the case. Such a latitude of construction would render unavailing every practical definition of particular and limited powers. Under the idea of preventing war in general, as well as invasion in particular, not only an indiscriminate removal of all aliens might be enforced, but a thousand other things, still more remote from the operations and precautions appurtenant to war, might take place. A bigoted or tyrannical nation might threaten us with war, unless certain religious or political regulations were adopted by us; yet it never could be inferred, if the regulations which would prevent war were such as Congress had otherwise no power to make, that the power to make them would grow out of the purpose they were to answer. Congress have power to suppress insurrections; yet it would not be allowed to follow, that they might employ all the means tending to prevent them; of which a system of moral instruction for the ignorant, and of provident support for the poor, might be regarded as among the most efficacious.

One argument for the power of the general government to remove aliens would have been passed in silence, if it had appeared under any authority inferior to that of a report made, during the last session of Congress, to the House of Representatives, by a committee, and approved by the house. The doctrine on which this argument is founded is of so new and so extraordinary a character, and strikes so radically at the political system of America, that it is proper to state it in the very words of the report.

"The act (concerning aliens) is said to be unconstitutional, because to remove aliens is a direct breach of the Constitution, which provides, by the 9th section of the 1st article, that the migration or importation of such persons as any of the states shall think proper to admit, shall not be prohibited by the Congress prior to the year 1808."

Among the answers given to this objection to the constitutionality of the act, the following very remarkable one is extracted:—

"Thirdly, That, as the Constitution has *given to the states* no power to remove aliens, during the period of the limitation under consideration, in the mean time, on the construction assumed, there would be no authority in the country empowered to send away dangerous aliens; which cannot be admitted."

The reasoning here used would not, in any view, be

conclusive; because there are powers exercised by most other governments, which, in the United States, are withheld by the people both from the general government and from the state governments. Of this sort are many of the powers prohibited by the declarations of rights prefixed to the constitutions, or by the clauses, in the constitutions, in the nature of such declarations. Nay, so far is the political system of the United States distinguishable from that of other countries, by the caution with which powers are delegated and defined, that, in one very important case, even of commercial regulation and revenue, the power is absolutely locked up against the hands of both governments. A tax on exports can be laid by no constitutional authority whatever. Under a system thus peculiarly guarded, there could surely be no absurdity in supposing that alien friends—who, if guilty of treasonable machinations, may be punished, or, if suspected on probable grounds, may be secured by pledges or imprisonment, in like manner with permanent citizens—were never meant to be subjected to banishment by an arbitrary and unusual process, either under the one government or the other.

But it is not the inconclusiveness of the general reasoning, in this passage, which chiefly calls the attention to it. It is the principle assumed by it, that the powers held by the states are given to them by the Constitution of the United States; and the inference from this principle, that the powers supposed to be necessary, which are not so given to the state governments, must reside in this government of the United States.

The respect which is felt for every portion of the constituted authorities forbids some of the reflections which this singular paragraph might excite; and they are the more readily suppressed, as it may be presumed, with justice perhaps as well as candor, that inadvertence may have had its share in the error. It would be unjustifiable delicacy, nevertheless, to pass by so portentous a claim, proceeding from so high an authority, without a monitory notice of the fatal tendencies with which it would be pregnant.

Lastly, it is said that a law on the same subject with the alien act, passed by this state originally in 1785, and reënacted in 1792, is a proof that a summary removal of suspected aliens was not heretofore regarded, by the Virginia legislature, as liable to the objections now urged against such a measure.

This charge against Virginia vanishes before the simple remark, that the law of Virginia relates to "suspicious persons, being the subjects of any foreign power or state who shall have *made a declaration of war,* or actually *commenced hostilities,* or from whom the President shall apprehend *hostile designs;*" whereas the act of Congress relates to aliens, being the subjects of foreign powers and states, who have *neither declared war, nor commenced hostilities, nor from whom hostile dangers are apprehended.*

2. It is next affirmed of the Alien Act, that it unites legislative, judicial, and executive powers, in the hands of the President.

However difficult it may be to mark, in every case, with clearness and certainty, the line which divides legislative power from the other departments of power, all will agree that the powers referred to these departments may be so general and undefined, as to be of a legislative, not of an executive or judicial nature, and may for that reason be unconstitutional. Details, to a certain degree, are essential to the nature and character of law; and on criminal subjects, it is proper that details should leave as little as possible to the discretion of those who are to apply and execute the law. If nothing more were required, in exercising a legislative trust, than a general conveyance of authority—without laying down any precise rules by which the authority conveyed should be carried into effect—it would follow that the whole power of legislation might be transferred by the legislature from itself, and proclamations might become substitutes for law. A delegation of power in this latitude would not be denied to be a union of the different powers.

To determine, then, whether the appropriate powers of the distinct departments are united by the act authorizing the executive to remove aliens, it must be inquired whether it contains such details, definitions, and rules, as appertain to the true character of a law; especially a law by which personal liberty is invaded, property deprived of its value to the owner, and life itself indirectly exposed to danger.

The Alien Act declares "that it shall be lawful for the President to order all such aliens as he shall judge *dangerous* to the peace and safety of the United States, or shall have reasonable ground to *suspect* are concerned in any treasonable or *secret machinations* against the government thereof, to depart," &c.

Could a power be well given in terms less definite, less particular, and less precise? To be *dangerous to the public safety*—to be *suspected of secret machination* against the government; these can never be mistaken for legal rules or certain definitions. They leave every thing to the President. His will is the law.

But it is not a legislative power only that is given to the President. He is to stand in the place of the judiciary also. His suspicion is the only evidence which is to convict; his order, the only judgment which is to be executed.

Thus it is the President whose will is to designate the offensive conduct; it is his will that is to ascertain the individuals on whom it is charged; and it is his will that is to cause the sentence to be executed. It is rightly affirmed, therefore, that the act unites legislative and judicial powers to those of the executive.

3. It is affirmed that this union of power subverts the general principle of free government.

It has become an axiom in the science of government, that a separation of the legislative, executive, and judicial departments is necessary to the preservation of public liberty. Nowhere has this axiom been better understood in theory, or more carefully pursued in practice, than in the United States.

4. It is affirmed that such a union of power subverts the particular organization and positive provision of the Federal Constitution.

According to the particular organization of the Constitution, its legislative powers are vested in the Congress, its executive powers in the President, and its judicial powers in a supreme and inferior tribunals. The union of any of these powers, and still more of all three, in any one of these departments, as has been shown to be done by the Alien Act, must, consequently, subvert the constitutional organization of them.

That positive provisions, in the Constitution, securing to individuals the benefits of fair trial, are also violated by the union of powers in the Alien Act, necessarily results from the two facts, that the act relates to alien friends, and that alien friends, being under the municipal law only, are entitled to its protection.

The *second* object, against which the resolution protests, is the Sedition Act.

Of this act it is affirmed—1. That it exercises, in like manner, a power not delegated by the Constitution; 2. That the power, on the contrary, is expressly and positively forbidden by one of the amendments to the Constitution; 3. That this is a power which, more than any other, ought to produce universal alarm, because it is levelled against that right of freely examining public characters and measures, and of free communication thereon, which has ever been justly deemed the only effectual guardian of every other right.

1. That it exercises a power not delegated by the Constitution.

Here, again, it will be proper to recollect that, the federal government being composed of powers specifically granted, with reservation of all others to the states or to the people, the positive authority under which the Sedition Act could be passed must be produced by those who assert its constitutionality. In what part of the Constitution, then, is this authority to be found?

Several attempts have been made to answer this question, which will be examined in their order. The committee will begin with one which has filled them with equal astonishment and apprehension; and which, they cannot but persuade themselves, must have the same effect on all who will consider it with coolness and impartiality, and with a reverence for our Constitution, in the true character in which it issued from the sovereign authority of the people. The committee refer to the doctrine lately advanced, as a sanction to the Sedition Act, "that the common or unwritten law"—a law of vast extent and complexity, and embracing almost every possible subject of legislation, both civil and criminal—makes a part of the law of these states, in their united and national capacity.

The novelty, and, in the judgment of the committee, the extravagance of this pretension, would have consigned it to the silence in which they have passed by other arguments which an extraordinary zeal for the act has drawn into the discussion; but the auspices under which this innovation presents itself have constrained the committee to bestow on it an attention which other considerations might have forbidden.

In executing the task, it may be of use to look back to the colonial state of this country prior to the revolution; to trace the effect of the revolution which converted the colonies into independent states; to inquire into the import of the Articles of Confederation, the first instrument by which the union of the states was regularly established; and, finally, to consult the Constitution of 1787, which is the oracle that must decide the important question.

In the state prior to the revolution, it is certain that the common law, under different limitations, made a part of the colonial codes. But, whether it be understood that the original colonists brought the law with them, or made it their law by adoption, it is equally certain that it was the separate law of each colony within its respective limits, and was unknown to them as a law pervading and operating through the whole, as one society.

It could not possibly be otherwise. The common law was not the same in any two of the colonies; in some, the modifications were materially and extensively different. There was no common legislature, by which a common will could be expressed in the form of a law; nor any common magistracy, by which such a law could be carried into practice. The will of each colony, alone and separately, had its organs for these purposes.

This stage of our political history furnishes no foothold for the patrons of this new doctrine.

Did, then, the principle or operation of the great event which made the colonies independent states, imply or introduce the common law, as a law of the Union?

The fundamental principle of the revolution was, that the colonies were coördinate members with each other, and with Great Britain, of an empire united by a common executive sovereign, but not united by any common legislative sovereign. The legislative power was maintained to be as complete in each American Parliament, as in the British Parliament. And the royal prerogative was in force, in each colony, by virtue of its acknowledging the king for its executive magistrate, as it was in Great Britain, by virtue of a like acknowledgment there. A denial of these principles by Great Britain, and the assertion of them by America, produced the revolution.

There was a time, indeed, when an exception to the legislative separation of the several component and coëqual parts of the empire obtained a degree of acquiescence. The British Parliament was allowed to regulate the trade with foreign nations, and between the different parts of the empire. This was, however, mere practice without right, and contrary to the true theory of the Constitution. The convenience of some regulations, in both cases, was apparent; and, as there was no legislature with power over the whole, nor any constitutional preëminence among the legislatures of the several parts, it was natural for the legislature of that particular part which was the eldest and the largest, to assume this function, and for the others to acquiesce in it. This tacit arrangement was the less criticised, as the regulations established by the British Parliament operated in favor of that part of the empire which seemed to bear the principal share of the public burdens, and were regarded as an indemnification of its advances for the other parts. As long as this regulating power was confined to the two objects of conveniency and equity, it was not complained of, nor much inquired into. But no sooner was it perverted to the selfish views of the party assuming it, than the injured parties began to feel and to reflect; and the moment the claim to a direct and indefinite power was ingrafted on the precedent of the regulating power, the whole charm was dissolved, and every eye opened to the usurpation. The assertion by Great Britain of a power to make laws for the other members of the empire, in all cases whatsoever, ended in the discovery that she had a right to make laws for them in no cases whatsoever.

Such being the ground of our revolution, no support or color can be drawn from it for the doctrine that the common law is binding on these states as one society. The doctrine, on the contrary, is evidently repugnant to the fundamental principle of the revolution.

The Articles of Confederation are the next source of information on this subject.

In the interval between the commencement of the revolution and the final ratification of these Articles, the nature and extent of the Union was determined by the circumstances of the crisis, rather than by any accurate delineation of the general authority. It will not be alleged that the "common law" could have any legitimate birth, as a law of the United States, during that state of things. If it came, as such, into existence at all, the charter of confederation must have been its parent.

Here, again, however, its pretensions are absolutely destitute of foundation. This instrument does not contain a sentence or a syllable that can be tortured into a countenance of the idea that the parties to it were, with respect to the objects of the common law, to form one community. No such law is named, or implied, or alluded to, as being in force, or as brought into force by that compact. No provision is made by which such a law could be carried into operation; whilst, on the other hand, every such inference or pretext is absolutely precluded by art. 2, which declares "that each state retains its sovereignty, freedom, and independence, and every power, jurisdiction, and right, which is not by this Confederation expressly delegated to the United States in Congress assembled."

Thus far it appears that not a vestige of this extraordinary doctrine can be found in the origin or progress of American institutions. The evidence against it has, on the contrary, grown stronger at every step, till it has amounted to a formal and positive exclusion, by written articles of compact among the parties concerned.

Is this exclusion revoked, and the common law introduced as national law, by the present Constitution of the United States? This is the final question to be examined.

It is readily admitted that particular parts of the common law may have a sanction from the Constitution, so far as they are necessarily comprehended in the technical phrases which express the powers delegated to the government; and so far, also, as such other parts may be adopted by Congress, as necessary and proper for carrying into execution the powers expressly delegated. But the question does not relate to either of these portions of the common law. It relates to the common law beyond these limitations.

The only part of the Constitution which seems to have been relied on in this case, is the 2d section of art. 3:—"The judicial power shall extend to all cases, in law and equity, arising under this Constitution, the laws of the United States, and treaties made, or which shall be made, under their authority."

It has been asked what cases, distinct from those arising under the laws and treaties of the United States, can arise under the Constitution, other than those arising under the common law; and it is inferred that the common law is, accordingly, adopted or recognized by the Constitution.

Never, perhaps, was so broad a construction applied to a text so clearly unsusceptible of it. If any color for the inference could be found, it must be in the impossibility of finding any other cases, in law and equity, within the provisions of the Constitution, to satisfy the expression; and rather than resort to a construction affecting so essentially the whole character of the government, it would perhaps be more rational to consider the expression as a mere pleonasm or inadvertence. But it is not necessary to decide on such a dilemma. The expression is fully satisfied, and its accuracy justified, by two descriptions of cases, to which the judicial authority is extended, and neither of which implies that the common law is the law of the United States. One of these descriptions comprehends the cases growing out of the restrictions on the legislative power of the states. For example, it is provided that "no state shall emit bills of credit," or "make any thing but gold and silver coin a tender for the payment of debts." Should this prohibition be violated, and a suit between citizens of the same state be the consequence, this would be a case arising under the Constitution before the judicial power of the United States. A second description comprehends suits between citizens and foreigners, of citizens of different states, to be decided according to the state or foreign laws, but submitted by the Constitution to the judicial power of the United States; the judicial power being, in several instances, extended beyond the legislative power of the United States.

To this explanation of the text, the following observations may be added:—

The expression "cases in law and equity" is manifestly confined to cases of a civil nature, and would exclude cases of criminal jurisdiction. Criminal cases in law and equity would be a language unknown to the law.

The succeeding paragraph in the same section is in harmony with this construction. It is in these words: "In all cases affecting ambassadors, or other public ministers, and consuls, and those in which a state shall be a party, the Supreme Court shall have original jurisdiction. *In all* the other cases, [including cases of law and equity arising under the Constitution,] the Supreme Court shall have *appellate* jurisdiction, both as to law and *fact,* with such exceptions, and under such regulations, as Congress shall make."

This paragraph, by expressly giving an *appellate* jurisdiction, in cases of law and equity arising under the Constitution, to *fact,* as well as to law, clearly excludes criminal cases, where the trial by jury is secured—because the fact, in such cases, is not a subject of appeal; and, although the appeal is liable to such *exceptions* and regulations as Congress may adopt, yet it is not to be supposed that an *exception* of *all* criminal cases could be contemplated, as well because a discretion in Congress to make or omit the exception would be improper, as because it would have been unnecessary. The exception could as easily have been made by the Constitution itself, as referred to the Congress.

Once more: The amendment last added to the Constitution deserves attention as throwing light on this subject. "The judicial power of the United States shall not be construed to extend to any suit in *law* or *equity,* commenced or prosecuted against one of the United States, by citizens of another state, or by citizens or subjects of any foreign power." As it will not be pretended that any criminal proceeding could take place against a state, the terms *law or equity* must be understood as appropriate to *civil,* in exclusion of *criminal* cases.

From these considerations, it is evident that this part of the Constitution, even if it could be applied at all to the purpose for which it has been cited, would not include any cases whatever of a criminal nature, and consequently would not authorize the inference from it, that the judicial authority extends to *offences* against the common law, as offences arising under the Constitution.

It is further to be considered that, even if this part of the Constitution could be strained into an application to every common-law case, criminal as well as civil, it could have no effect in justifying the Sedition Act, which is an act of legislative, and not of judicial power: and it is the judicial power only of which the extent is defined in this part of the Constitution.

There are two passages in the Constitution, in which a description of the law of the United States is found. The first is contained in art. 3, sect. 3, in the words following: "This Constitution, the laws of the United States, and treaties made, or which shalt be made, under this authority." The second is contained in the second paragraph of art. 6, as follows: "This Constitution, and the laws of the United States which shall be made in pursuance thereof, and all treaties made, or which shall be made, under the authority of the United States, shall be the supreme law of the land." The first of these descriptions was meant as a guide to the judges of the United States; the second, as a guide to the judges of the several states. Both of them consist of an enumeration, which was evidently meant to be precise and complete. If the common law had been understood to be a law of the United States, it is not possible to assign a satisfactory reason why it was not expressed in the enumeration.

In aid of these objections, the difficulties and confusion

inseparable from a constructive introduction of the common law would afford powerful reasons against it.

Is it to be the common law with or without the British statutes?

If without the statutory amendments, the vices of the code would be insupportable.

If with these amendments, what period is to be fixed for limiting the British authority over our laws?

Is it to be the date of the eldest, or the youngest, of the colonies?

Or are the dates to be thrown together, and a medium deduced?

Or is our independence to be taken for the date?

Is, again, regard to be had to the various changes in the common law made by the local codes of America?

Is regard to be had to such changes subsequent as well as prior to the establishment of the Constitution?

Is regard to be had to future as well as past changes?

Is the law to be different in every state, as differently modified by its code; or are the modifications of any particular state to be applied to all?

And on the latter supposition, which among the state codes forms the standard?

Questions of this sort might be multiplied with as much ease as there would be difficulty in answering them.

These consequences, flowing from the proposed construction, furnish other objections equally conclusive; unless the text were peremptory in its meaning, and consistent with other parts of the instrument.

These consequences may be in relation to the legislative

authority of the United States; to the executive authority; to the judicial authority; and to the governments of the several states.

If it be understood that the common law is established by the Constitution, it follows that no part of the law can be altered by the legislature. Such of the statutes already passed as may be repugnant thereto, would be nullified; particularly the Sedition Act itself, which boasts of being a melioration of the common law; and the whole code, with all its incongruities, barbarisms, and bloody maxims, would be inviolably saddled on the good people of the United States.

Should this consequence be rejected, and the common law be held, like other laws, liable to revision and alteration by the authority of Congress, it then follows that the authority of Congress is coëxtensive with the objects of common law; that is to say, with every object of legislation; for to every such object does some branch or other of the common law extend. The authority of Congress would, therefore, be no longer under the limitations marked out in the Constitution. They would be authorized to legislate in all cases whatsoever.

In the next place, as the President possesses the executive powers of the Constitution, and is to see that the laws be faithfully executed, his authority also must be coëxtensive with every branch of the common law. The additions which this would make to his power, though not readily to be estimated, claim the most serious attention.

This is not all: it will merit the most profound consideration, how far an indefinite admission of the common law, with a latitude in construing it equal to the construction by which it is deduced from the Constitution, might draw after it the various prerogatives, making part of the unwritten law of England. The English constitution itself is nothing more than a composition of unwritten laws and maxims.

In the third place, whether the common law be admitted as of legal or of constitutional obligation, it would confer on the judicial department a discretion little short of a legislative power.

On the supposition of its having a constitutional obligation, this power in the judges would be permanent and irremediable by the legislature. On the other supposition, the power would not expire until the legislature should have introduced a full system of statutory provisions. Let it be observed, too, that, besides all the uncertainties above enumerated, and which present an immense field for judicial discretion, it would remain with the same department to decide what parts of the common law would, and what would not, be properly applicable to the circumstances of the United States.

A discretion of this sort has always been lamented as incongruous and dangerous, even in the colonial and state courts, although so much narrowed by positive provisions in the local codes on all the principal subjects embraced by the common law. Under the United States, where so few laws exist on those subjects, and where so great a lapse of time must happen before the vast chasm could be supplied, it is manifest that the power of the judges over the law would, in fact, erect them into legislators, and that, for a long time, it would be impossible for the citizens to conjecture either what was, or would be, law.

In the last place, the consequence of admitting the common law as the law of the United States, on the authority of the individual states, is as obvious as it would be fatal. As this law relates to every subject of legislation, and would be paramount to the constitutions and laws of the states, the admission of it would overwhelm the residuary sovereignty of the states, and, by one constructive operation, new-model the whole political fabric of the country.

From the review thus taken of the situation of the American colonies prior to their independence; of the effect of this event on their situation; of the nature and import of the Articles of Confederation; of the true meaning of the passage in the existing Constitution from which the common law has been deduced; of the difficulties and uncertainties incident to the doctrine; and of its vast consequences in extending the powers of the federal government, and in superseding the authorities of the state governments,—the committee feel the utmost confidence in concluding that the common law never was, nor by any fair construction ever can be, deemed a law for the American people as one community; and they indulge the strongest expectation that the same conclusion will be finally drawn by all candid and accurate inquirers into the subject. It is, indeed, distressing to reflect that it ever should have been made a question, whether the Constitution, on the whole face of which is seen so much labor to enumerate and define the several objects of federal power, could intend to introduce in the lump, in an indirect manner, and by a forced construction of a few phrases, the vast and multifarious jurisdiction involved in the common law—a law filling so many ample volumes; a law overspreading the entire field of legislation; and a law that would sap the foundation of the Constitution as a system of limited and specified powers. A severer reproach could not, in the opinion of the committee, be thrown on the Constitution, on those who framed, or on those who established it, than such a supposition would throw on them.

The argument, then, drawn from the common law, on the ground of its being adopted or recognized by the Constitution, being inapplicable to the Sedition Act, the committee will proceed to examine the other arguments which have been founded on the Constitution.

They will waste but little time on the attempt to cover the act by the preamble to the Constitution, it being contrary to every acknowledged rule of construction to set up this part of an instrument in opposition to the plain meaning expressed in the body of the instrument. A preamble usually contains the general motives or reason for the particular regulations or measures which follow it, and is always understood to be explained and limited by them. In the present instance, a contrary interpretation would have the inadmissible effect of rendering nugatory or improper every part of the Constitution which succeeds the preamble.

The paragraph in art. 1, sect. 8, which contains the power to lay and collect taxes, duties, imposts, and excises, to pay the debts, and provide for the common defence and general welfare, having been already examined, will also require no particular attention in this place. It will have been seen that, in its fair and consistent meaning, it cannot enlarge the enumerated powers vested in Congress.

The part of the Constitution which seems most to be recurred to, in defence of the Sedition Act, is the last clause of the above section, empowering Congress to make all laws which shall be necessary and proper for carrying into execution the foregoing powers, and all other powers vested by this Constitution in the government of the United States, or in any department or officer thereof."

The plain import of this clause is, that Congress shall have all the incidental or instrumental powers necessary and proper for carrying into execution all the express powers, whether they be vested in the government of the United States, more collectively, or in the several departments or officers thereof.

It is not a grant of new powers to Congress, but merely a declaration, for the removal of all uncertainty, that the means of carrying into execution those otherwise granted are included in the grant.

Whenever, therefore, a question arises concerning the constitutionality of a particular power, the first question is, whether the power be expressed in the Constitution. If it be, the question is decided. If it be not expressed, the next inquiry must be, whether it is properly an incident to an express power, and necessary to its execution. If it be, it may be exercised by Congress. If it be not, Congress cannot exercise it.

Let the question be asked, then, whether the power over the press, exercised in the Sedition Act, be found among the powers expressly vested in Congress. This is not pretended.

Is there any express power, for executing which it is a necessary and proper power?

The power which has been selected, as least remote, in answer to this question, is that "of suppressing insurrections;" which is said to imply a power to prevent insurrections, by punishing whatever may lead or tend to them. But it surely cannot, with the least plausibility, be said, that the regulation of the press, and punishment of libels, are exercises of a power to suppress insurrections. The most that could be said would be, that the punishment of libels, if it had the tendency ascribed to it, might prevent the occasion of passing or executing laws necessary and proper for the suppression of insurrections.

Has the federal government no power, then, to prevent as well as to punish resistance to the laws?

They have the power, which the Constitution deemed most proper, in their hands for the purpose. The Congress has power, before it happens, to pass laws for punishing it; and the executive and judiciary have power to enforce those laws when it does happen.

It must be recollected by many, and could be shown to the satisfaction of all, that the construction here put on the terms "necessary and proper" is precisely the construction which prevailed during the discussions and ratifications of the Constitution. It may be added, and cannot too often be repeated, that it is a construction absolutely necessary to maintain their consistency with the peculiar character of the government, as possessed of particular and definite powers only, not of the general and indefinite powers vested in ordinary governments; for, if the power to suppress insurrections includes the power to punish libels, or if the power to punish includes a power to prevent, by all the means that may have that tendency, such is the relation and influence among the most remote subjects of legislation, that a power over a very few would carry with it a power over all. And it must be wholly immaterial whether unlimited powers be exercised under the name of unlimited powers, or be exercised under the name of unlimited means of carrying into execution limited powers.

This branch of the subject will be closed with a reflection which must have weight with all, but more especially with those who place peculiar reliance on the judicial exposition of the Constitution, as the bulwark provided against an undue extension of the legislative power. If it be understood that the powers implied in the specified powers have an immediate and appropriate relation to them, as means necessary and proper for carrying them into execution, questions on constitutionality of laws passed for this purpose will be of a nature sufficiently precise and determinate for judicial cognizance and control. If, on the other hand, Congress are not limited, in the choice of means, by any such appropriate relation of them to the specified powers, but may employ all such means as they may deem fitted to prevent, as well as to punish, crimes subjected to their authority, (such as may have a tendency only to promote an object for which they are authorized to provide,) every one must perceive that questions relating to means of this sort must be questions for mere policy and expediency; on which legislative discretion alone can decide, and from which the judicial interposition and control are completely excluded.

2. The next point which the resolution requires to be proved is, that the power over the press, exercised by the Sedition Act, is positively forbidden by one of the amendments to the Constitution.

The amendment stands in these words: "Congress shall

make no law respecting an establishment of religion, or prohibiting the free exercise thereof, or abridging the freedom of speech, or of the press, or of the right of the people peaceably to assemble, and to petition the government for a redress of grievances."

In the attempts to vindicate the Sedition Act, it has been contended, 1. That the "freedom of the press" is to be determined by the meaning of these terms in the common law; 2. That the article supposes the power over the press to be in Congress, and prohibits them only from abridging the freedom allowed to it by the common law.

Although it will be shown, on examining the second of these positions, that the amendment is a denial to Congress of all power over the press, it may not be useless to make the following observations on the first of them:—

It is deemed to be a sound opinion that the Sedition Act, in its definition of some of the crimes created, is an abridgment of the freedom of publication, recognized by principles of the common law in England.

The freedom of the press, under the common law, is, in the defences of the Sedition Act, made to consist in an exemption from all previous restraint on printed publications, by persons authorized to inspect or prohibit them. It appears to the committee that this idea of the freedom of the press can never be admitted to be the American idea of it; since a law inflicting penalties on printed publications would have a similar effect with a law authorizing a previous restraint on them. It would seem a mockery to say that no laws should be passed preventing publications from being made, but that laws might be passed for punishing them in case they should be made.

The essential difference between the British government and the American constitutions will place this subject in the clearest light.

In the British government, the danger of encroachments on the rights of the people is understood to be confined to the executive magistrate. The representatives of the people in the legislature are not only exempt themselves from distrust, but are considered as sufficient guardians of the rights of their constituents against the danger from the executive. Hence it is a principle, that the Parliament is unlimited in its power; or, in their own language, is omnipotent. Hence, too, all the ramparts for protecting the rights of the people,—such as their Magna Charta, their bill of rights, &c.,—are not reared against the Parliament, but against the royal prerogative. They are merely legislative precautions against executive usurpation. Under such a government as this, an exemption of the press from previous restraint by licensers appointed by the king, is all the freedom that can be secured to it.

In the United States, the case is altogether different. The people, not the government, possess the absolute sovereignty. The legislature, no less than the executive, is under limitations of power. Encroachments are regarded as possible from the one as well as from the other. Hence, in the United States, the great and essential rights of the people are secured against legislative as well as executive ambition. They are secured, not by laws paramount to prerogative, but by constitutions paramount to laws. This security of the freedom of the press requires that it should be exempt, not only from previous restraint of the executive, as in Great Britain, but from legislative restraint also; and this exemption, to be effectual, must be an exemption, not only from the previous inspection of licensers, but from the subsequent penalty of laws.

The state of the press, therefore, under the common law, cannot, in this point of view, be the standard of its freedom in the United States.

But there is another view under which it may be necessary to consider this subject. It may be alleged that, although the security for the freedom of the press be different in Great Britain and in this country,—being a legal security only in the former, and a constitutional security in the latter,—and although there may be a further difference, in an extension of the freedom of the press, here, beyond an exemption from previous restraint, to an exemption from subsequent penalties also,—yet the actual legal freedom of the press, under the common law, must determine the degree of freedom which is meant by the terms, and which is constitutionally secured against both previous and subsequent restraints.

The committee are not unaware of the difficulty of all general questions, which may turn on the proper boundary between the liberty and licentiousness of the press. They will leave it, therefore, for consideration only, how far the difference between the nature of the British government, and the nature of the American government, and the practice under the latter, may show the degree of rigor in the former to be inapplicable to, and not obligatory in, the latter.

The nature of governments elective, limited, and responsible, in all their branches, may well be supposed to require a greater freedom of animadversion, than might be tolerated by the genius of such a government as that of Great Britain. In the latter, it is a maxim, that the king—an hereditary, not a responsible magistrate—can do no wrong; and that the legislature, which, in two thirds of its composition, is also hereditary, not responsible, can do what it pleases. In the United States, the executive magistrates are not held to be infallible, nor the legislatures to be omnipotent; and both, being elective, are both responsible. Is it not natural and necessary, under such different circumstances, that a different degree of freedom in the use of the press should be contemplated?

Is not such an inference favored by what is observable in Great Britain itself? Notwithstanding the general doctrine of the common law, on the subject of the press, and the occasional punishment of those who use it with a freedom offensive to the government, it is well known that, with respect to the responsible measures of the government, where the reasons operating here become applicable there, the freedom exercised by the press, and protected by public opinion, far exceeds the limits prescribed by the ordinary rules of law. The ministry, who are responsible to impeachment, are at all times animadverted on, by the press, with peculiar freedom; and during the elections for the House of Commons, the other responsible part of the government, the press is employed with as little reserve towards the candidates.

The practice in America must be entitled to much more respect. In every state, probably, in the Union, the press has exerted a freedom in canvassing the merits and measures of public men, of every description, which has not been confined to the strict limits of the common law. On this footing the freedom of the press has stood; on this foundation it yet stands; and it will not be a breach, either of truth or of candor, to say that no persons or presses are in the habit of more unrestrained animadversions on the proceedings and functionaries of the state governments, than the persons and presses most zealous in vindicating the act of Congress for punishing similar animadversions on the government of the United States.

The last remark will not be understood as claiming for the state governments an immunity greater than they have heretofore enjoyed. Some degree of abuse is inseparable from the proper use of every thing; and in no instance is this more true than in that of the press. It has accordingly been decided, by the practice of the states, that it is better to leave a few of its noxious branches to their luxuriant growth, than, by pruning them away, to injure the vigor of those yielding the proper fruits. And can the wisdom of this policy be doubted by any one who reflects that to the press alone, checkered as it is with abuses, the world is indebted for all the triumphs which have been gained by reason and humanity over error and oppression; who reflects that to the same beneficent source the United States owe much of the lights which conducted them to the rank of a free and independent nation and which have improved their political system into a shape so auspicious to their happiness? Had Sedition Acts, forbidding every publication that might bring the constituted agents into contempt or disrepute, or that might excite the hatred of the people against the authors of unjust or pernicious measures, been uniformly enforced against the press, might not the United States have been languishing, at this day, under the infirmities of a sickly Confederation? Might they not, possibly, be miserable colonies, groaning under a foreign yoke?

To these observations one fact will be added, which demonstrates that the common law cannot be admitted as the universal expositor of American terms, which may be the same with those contained in that law. The freedom of conscience, and of religion, is found in the same instrument which asserts the freedom of the press. It will never be admitted that the meaning of the former, in the common law of England, is to limit their meaning in the United States.

Whatever weight may be allowed to these considerations, the committee do not, however, by any means intend to rest the question on them. They contend that the article of the amendment, instead of supposing in Congress a power that might be exercised over the press, provided its freedom was not abridged, meant a positive denial to Congress of any power whatever on the subject.

To demonstrate that this was the true object of the article, it will be sufficient to recall the circumstances which led to it, and to refer to the explanation accompanying the article.

When the Constitution was under the discussions which preceded its ratification, it is well known that great apprehensions were expressed by many, lest the omission of some positive exception, from the powers delegated, of certain rights, and of the freedom of the press particularly, might expose them to danger of being drawn, by construction, within some of the powers vested in Congress; more especially of the power to make all laws necessary and proper for carrying their other powers into execution. In reply to this objection, it was invariably urged to be a fundamental and characteristic principle of the Constitution, that all powers not given by it were reserved; that no powers were given beyond those enumerated in the Constitution, and such as were fairly incident to them; that the power over the rights in question, and particularly over the press, was neither among the enumerated powers, nor incident to any of them: and consequently that an exercise of any such power would be manifest usurpation. It is painful to remark how much the arguments now employed in behalf of the Sedition Act, are at variance with the reasoning which then justified the Constitution, and invited its ratification.

From this posture of the subject resulted the interesting question, in so many of the conventions, whether the doubts and dangers ascribed to the Constitution should be removed by any amendments previous to the ratification, or be postponed, in confidence that, as far as they might be proper, they would be introduced in the form provided by the Constitution. The latter course was adopted; and in most of the states, ratifications were followed by the propositions and instructions for rendering the Constitution more explicit, and more safe to the rights not meant to be delegated by it. Among those rights, the freedom of the press, in most instances, is particularly and emphatically mentioned. The firm and very pointed manner in which it is asserted in the proceedings of the Convention of this state will hereafter be seen.

In pursuance of the wishes thus expressed, the first

Congress that assembled under the Constitution proposed certain amendments, which have since, by the necessary ratifications, been made a part of it; among which amendments is the article containing, among other prohibitions on the Congress, an express declaration that they should make no law abridging the freedom of the press.

Without tracing farther the evidence on this subject, it would seem scarcely possible to doubt that no power whatever over the press was supposed to be delegated by the Constitution, as it originally stood, and that the amendment was intended as a positive and absolute reservation of it.

But the evidence is still stronger. The proposition of amendments made by Congress is introduced in the following terms:—

"The conventions of a number of the states having, at the time of their adopting the Constitution, expressed a desire, in order to prevent misconstruction or abuse of its powers, that further declaratory and restrictive clauses should be added; and as extending the ground of public confidence in the government will best insure the beneficent ends of its institutions."

Here is the most satisfactory and authentic proof that the several amendments proposed were to be considered as either declaratory or restrictive, and, whether the one or the other, as corresponding with the desire expressed by a number of the states, and as extending the ground of public confidence in the government.

Under any other construction of the amendment relating to the press, than that it declared the press to be wholly exempt from the power of Congress, the amendment could neither be said to correspond with the desire expressed by a number of the states, nor be calculated to extend the ground of public confidence in the government.

Nay, more; the construction employed to justify the Sedition Act would exhibit a phenomenon without a parallel in the political world. It would exhibit a number of respectable states, as denying, first, that any power over the press was delegated by the Constitution; as proposing, next, that an amendment to it should explicitly declare that no such power was delegated; and, finally, as concurring in an amendment actually recognizing or delegating such a power.

Is, then, the federal government, it will be asked, destitute of every authority for restraining the licentiousness of the press, and for shielding itself against the libellous attacks which may be made on those who administer it?

The Constitution alone can answer this question. If no such power be expressly delegated, and if it be not both necessary and proper to carry into execution an express power; above all, if it be expressly forbidden, by a declaratory amendment to the Constitution,—the answer must be, that the federal government is destitute of all such authority.

And might it not be asked, in turn, whether it is not more probable, under all the circumstances which have been reviewed, that the authority should be withheld by the Constitution, than that it should be left to a vague and violent construction, whilst so much pains were bestowed in enumerating other powers, and so many less important powers are included in the enumeration?

Might it not be likewise asked, whether the anxious circumspection which dictated so many peculiar limitations on the general authority would be unlikely to exempt the press altogether from that authority? The peculiar magnitude of some of the powers necessarily committed to the federal government; the peculiar duration required for the functions of some of its departments; the peculiar distance of the seat of its proceedings from the great body of its constituents; and the peculiar difficulty of circulating an adequate knowledge of them through any other channel;—will not these considerations, some or other of which produced other exceptions from the powers of ordinary governments, altogether, account for the policy of binding the hands of the federal government from touching the channel which alone can give efficacy to its responsibility to its constituents, and of leaving those who administer it to a remedy, for their injured reputations, under the same laws, and in the same tribunals, which protect their lives, their liberties, and their properties?

But the question does not turn either on the wisdom of the Constitution or on the policy which gave rise to its particular organization. It turns on the actual meaning of the instrument, by which it has appeared that a power over the press is clearly excluded from the number of powers delegated to the federal government.

3. And, in the opinion of the committee, well may it be said, as the resolution concludes with saying, that the unconstitutional power exercised over the press by the Sedition Act ought, "more than any other, to produce universal alarm; because it is levelled against that right of freely examining public characters and measures, and of free com-

munication among the people thereon, which has ever been justly deemed the only effectual guardian of every other right."

Without scrutinizing minutely into all the provisions of the Sedition Act, it will be sufficient to cite so much of section 2d as follows:—"And be it further enacted, that if any shall write, print, utter, or publish, or shall cause or procure to be written, printed, uttered, or published, or shall knowingly and willingly assist or aid in writing, printing, uttering, or publishing, any false, scandalous, and malicious writing or writings against the government of the United States, or either house of the Congress of the United States, with an intent to defame the said government, or either house of the said Congress, or the President, or to bring them or either of them into contempt or disrepute, or to excite against them, or either or any of them, the hatred of the good people of the United States, &c.,—then such persons, being thereof convicted before any court of the United States having jurisdiction thereof, shall be punished by a fine not exceeding two thousand dollars, and by imprisonment not exceeding two years."

On this part of the act, the following observations present themselves:—

1. The Constitution supposes that the President, the Congress, and each of its Houses, may not discharge their trusts, either from defect of judgment or other causes. Hence they are all made responsible to their constituents, at the returning periods of elections; and the President, who is singly in-

trusted with very great powers, is, as a further guard, subjected to an intermediate impeachment.

2. Should it happen, as the Constitution supposes it may happen, that either of these branches of the government may not have duly discharged its trust, it is natural and proper, that, according to the cause and degree of their faults, they should be brought into contempt or disrepute, and incur the hatred of the people.
3. Whether it has, in any case, happened that the proceedings of either or all of those branches evince such a violation of duty as to justify a contempt, a disrepute, or hatred among the people, can only be determined by a free examination thereof, and a free communication among the people thereon.
4. Whenever it may have actually happened that proceedings of this sort are chargeable on all or either of the branches of the government, it is the duty, as well as the right, of intelligent and faithful citizens to discuss and promulgate them freely—as well to control them by the censorship of the public opinion, as to promote a remedy according to the rules of the Constitution. And it cannot be avoided that those who are to apply the remedy must feel, in some degree, a contempt or hatred against the transgressing party.
5. As the act was passed on July 14, 1798, and is to be in force until March 3, 1801, it was of course that, during its continuance, two elections of the entire House of Representatives, an election of a part of

the Senate, and an election of a President, were to take place.

6. That, consequently, during all these elections,—intended, by the Constitution, to preserve the purity or to purge the faults of the administration,—the great remedial rights of the people were to be exercised, and the responsibility of their public agents to be screened, under the penalties of this act.

May it not be asked of every intelligent friend to the liberties of his country, whether the power exercised in such an act as this ought not to produce great and universal alarm? Whether a rigid execution of such an act, in time past, would not have repressed that information and communication among the people which is indispensable to the just exercise of their electoral rights? And whether such an act, if made perpetual, and enforced with rigor, would not, in time to come, either destroy our free system of government, or prepare a convulsion that might prove equally fatal to it?

In answer to such questions, it has been pleaded that the writings and publications forbidden by the act are those only which are false and malicious, and intended to defame; and merit is claimed for the privilege allowed to authors to justify, by proving the truth of their publications, and for the limitations to which the sentence of fine and imprisonment is subjected.

To those who concurred in the act, under the extraordinary belief that the option lay between the passing of such an act, and leaving in force the common law of libels, which punishes truth equally with falsehood, and submits fine and imprisonment to the indefinite discretion of the court, the merit of good intentions ought surely not to be refused. A like merit may perhaps be due for the discontinuance of the corporal punishment, which the common law also leaves to the discretion of the court. This merit of intention, however, would have been greater, if the several mitigations had not been limited to so short a period; and the apparent inconsistency would have been avoided, between justifying the act, at one time, by contrasting it with the rigors of the common law otherwise in force; and at another time, by appealing to the nature of the crisis, as requiring the temporary rigor exerted by the act.

But, whatever may have been the meritorious intentions of all or any who contributed to the Sedition Act, a very few reflections will prove that its baleful tendency is little diminished by the privilege of giving in evidence the truth of the matter contained in political writings.

In the first place, where simple and naked facts alone are in question, there is sufficient difficulty in some cases, and sufficient trouble and vexation in all, in meeting a prosecution from the government with the full and formal proof necessary in a court of law.

But in the next place, it must be obvious to the plainest minds, that opinions and inferences, and conjectural observations, are not only in many cases inseparable from the facts, but may often be more the objects of the prosecution than the facts themselves; or may even be altogether abstracted from particular facts; and that opinion, and inferences, and conjectural observations, cannot be subjects of that kind of proof which appertains to facts, before a court of law.

Again: it is no less obvious that the intent to defame, or bring into contempt, or disrepute, or hatred,—which is made a condition of the offence created by the act,—cannot prevent its pernicious influence on the freedom of the press. For, omitting the inquiry, how far the malice of the intent is an inference of the law from the mere publication, it is manifestly impossible to punish the intent to bring those who administer the government into disrepute or contempt, without striking at the right of freely discussing public characters and measures; because those who engage in such discussions must expect and intend to excite these unfavorable sentiments, so far as they may be thought to be deserved. To prohibit the intent to excite those unfavorable sentiments against those who administer the government, is equivalent to a prohibition of the actual excitement of them; and to prohibit the actual excitement of them is equivalent to a prohibition of discussions having that tendency and effect; which, again, is equivalent to a protection of those who administer the government, if they should at any time deserve the contempt or hatred of the people, against being exposed to it, by free animadversions on their characters and conduct. Nor can there be a doubt, if those in public trust be shielded by penal laws from such strictures of the press as may expose them to contempt, or disrepute, or hatred, where they may deserve it, that, in exact proportion as they may deserve to be exposed, will be the certainty and criminality of the intent to expose them, and the vigilance of prosecuting and punishing it; nor a doubt that a government thus intrenched in penal statutes against the just and natural effects of a culpable administration, will easily evade the responsibility which is essential to a faithful discharge of its duty.

Let it be recollected, lastly, that the right of electing the members of the government constitutes more particularly the essence of a free and responsible government. The value and efficacy of this right depends on the knowledge of the comparative merits and demerits of the candidates for public trust, and on the equal freedom, consequently, of examining and discussing these merits and demerits of the candidates respectively. It has been seen that a number of important elections will take place while the act is in force although it should not be continued beyond the term to which it is limited. Should there happen, then, as is extremely probable in relation to some one or other of the branches of the government, to be competitions between those who are, and those who are not, members of the government, what will be the situations of the competitors? Not equal; because the characters of the former will be covered by the Sedition Act from animadversions exposing them to disrepute among the people, whilst the latter may be exposed to the contempt and hatred of the people without a violation of the act. What will be the situation of the people? Not free; because they will be compelled to make their election between competitors whose pretensions they are not permitted by the act equally to examine, to discuss, and to ascertain. And from both these situations will not those in power derive an undue advantage for continuing themselves in it; which, by impairing the right of election, endangers the blessings of the government founded on it?

It is with justice, therefore, that the General Assembly have affirmed, in the resolution, as well that the right of freely examining public characters and measures, and of communication thereon, is the only effectual guardian of every other right, as that this particular right is levelled at by the power exercised in the Sedition Act.

The resolution *next* in order is as follows:—

> "That this state having, by its Convention, which ratified the Federal Constitution, expressly declared that, among other essential rights, 'the liberty of conscience and of the press cannot be cancelled, abridged, restrained, or modified, by any authority of the United States;' and, from its extreme anxiety to guard these rights from every possible attack of sophistry and ambition, having, with other states, recommended an amendment for that purpose, which amendment was in due time annexed to the Constitution, it would mark a reproachful inconsistency, and criminal degeneracy, if an indifference were now shown to the most palpable violation of one of the rights thus declared and secured, and to the establishment of a precedent which may be fatal to the other."

To place this resolution in its just light, it will be necessary to recur to the act of ratification by Virginia, which stands in the ensuing form:—

> "We, the delegates of the people of Virginia, duly elected in pursuance of a recommendation from the General Assembly, and now met in Convention, having

> fully and freely investigated and discussed the proceedings of the Federal Convention, and being prepared, as well as the most mature deliberation hath enabled us, to decide thereon,—DO, in the name and in behalf of the people of Virginia, declare and make known, that the powers granted under the Constitution, being derived from the people of the United States, may be resumed by them whensoever the same shall be perverted to their injury or oppression; and that every power not granted thereby remains with them, and at their will. That, therefore, no right of any denomination can be cancelled, abridged, restrained, or modified, by the Congress, by the Senate or the House of Representatives, acting in any capacity, by the President, or any department or officer of the United States, except in those instances in which power is given by the Constitution for those purposes; and that, among other essential rights, the liberty of conscience and of the press cannot be cancelled, abridged, restrained, or modified, by any authority of the United States."

Here is an express and solemn declaration by the Convention of the state, that they ratified the Constitution in the sense that no right of any denomination can be cancelled, abridged, restrained, or modified, by the government of the United States, or any part of it, except in those instances in which power is given by the Constitution; and in the sense, particularly, "that among other essential rights, the liberty of conscience and freedom of the press cannot be cancelled, abridged, restrained, or modified, by any authority of the United States."

Words could not well express, in a fuller or more forcible manner, the understanding of the Convention, that the liberty of conscience and freedom of the press were *equally* and *completely* exempted from all authority whatever of the United States.

Under an anxiety to guard more effectually these rights against every possible danger, the Convention, after ratifying the Constitution, proceeded to prefix to certain amendments proposed by them, a declaration of rights, in which are two articles providing, the one for the liberty of conscience, the other for the freedom of speech and of the press.

Similar recommendations having proceeded from a number of other states; and Congress, as has been seen, having, in consequence thereof, and with a view to extend the ground of public confidence, proposed among other declaratory and restrictive clauses, a clause expressly securing the liberty of conscience and of the press; and Virginia having concurred in the ratifications which made them a part of the Constitution,—it will remain with a candid public to decide whether it would not mark an inconsistency and degeneracy, if an indifference were now shown to a palpable violation of one of those rights—the freedom of the press; and to a precedent, therein, which may be fatal to the other—the free exercise of religion.

That the precedent established by the violation of the former of these rights may, as is affirmed by the resolution, be fatal to the latter, appears to be demonstrable by a comparison of the grounds on which they respectively rest, and from the scope of reasoning by which the power of the former has been vindicated.

First, Both of these rights, the liberty of conscience, and of the press, rest equally on the original ground of not being delegated by the Constitution, and consequently withheld from the government. Any construction, therefore, that would attack this original security for the one, must have the like effect on the other.

Secondly, They are both equally secured by the supplement to the Constitution; being both included in the same amendment, made at the same time and by the same authority. Any construction or argument, then, which would turn the amendment into a grant or acknowledgment of power, with respect to the press, might be equally applied to the freedom of religion.

Thirdly, If it be admitted that the extent of the freedom of the press, secured by the amendment, is to be measured by the common law on this subject, the same authority may be resorted to for the standard which is to fix the extent of the "free exercise of religion." It cannot be necessary to say what this standard would be—whether the common law be taken solely as the unwritten, or as varied by the written law of England.

Fourthly, If the words and phrases in the amendment are to be considered as chosen with a studied discrimination, which yields an argument for a power over the press, under the limitation that its freedom be not abridged, the same argument results from the same consideration, for a power over the

> exercise of religion, under the limitation that its freedom be not prohibited.

For, if Congress may regulate the freedom of the press, provided they do not abridge it, because it is said only, "they shall not abridge it," and is not said "they shall make no law respecting it," the analogy of reasoning is conclusive, that Congress may *regulate,* and even *abridge,* the free exercise of religion, provided they do not *prohibit it;* because it is said only, "they shall not prohibit it;" and is *not* said, "they shall make no law *respecting,* or no law *abridging* it."

The General Assembly were governed by the clearest reason, then, in considering the Sedition Act, which legislates on the freedom of the press, as establishing a precedent that may be fatal to the liberty of conscience; and it will be the duty of all, in proportion as they value the security of the latter, to take the alarm at every encroachment on the former.

The two concluding resolutions only remain to be examined. They are in the words following:—

> "That the good people of this commonwealth, having ever felt, and continuing to feel, the most sincere affection for their brethren of the other states, the truest anxiety for establishing and perpetuating the union of all, and the most scrupulous fidelity to that Constitution which is the pledge of mutual friendship and the instrument of mutual happiness,—the General Assembly doth solemnly appeal to the like dispositions in the

other states, in confidence that they will concur with this commonwealth in declaring, as it does hereby declare, that the acts aforesaid are unconstitutional; and that the necessary and proper measures will be taken, by each, for coöperating with this state, in maintaining, unimpaired, the authorities, rights, and liberties, reserved to the states respectively, or to the people.

"That the governor be desired to transmit a copy of the foregoing resolutions to the executive authority of each of the other states, with a request that the same may be communicated to the legislature thereof; and that a copy be furnished to each of the senators and representatives representing this state in the Congress of the United States."

The fairness and regularity of the course of proceeding here pursued, have not protected it against objections even from sources too respectable to be disregarded.

It has been said that it belongs to the judiciary of the United States, and not the state legislatures, to declare the meaning of the Federal Constitution.

But a declaration that proceedings of the federal government are not warranted by the Constitution, is a novelty neither among the citizens nor among the legislatures of the states; nor are the citizens or the legislature of Virginia singular in the example of it.

Nor can the declarations of either, whether affirming or denying the constitutionality of measures of the federal government, or whether made before or after judicial decisions thereon, be deemed, in any point of view, an assumption of the office of the judge. The declarations in such cases are expressions of opinion, unaccompanied with any other effect than what they may produce on opinion, by exciting reflection. The expositions of the judiciary, on the other hand, are carried into immediate effect by force. The former may lead to a change in the legislative expression of the general will—possibly to a change in the opinion of the judiciary; the latter enforces the general will, whilst that will and that opinion continue unchanged.

And if there be no impropriety in declaring the unconstitutionality of proceedings in the federal government, where can there be the impropriety of communicating the declaration to other states, and inviting their concurrence in a like declaration? What is allowable for one, must be allowable for all; and a free communication among the states, where the Constitution imposes no restraint, is as allowable among the state governments as among other public bodies or private citizens. This consideration derives a weight that cannot be denied to it, from the relation of the state legislatures to the federal legislature as the immediate constituents of one of its branches.

The legislatures of the states have a right also to originate amendments to the Constitution, by a concurrence of two thirds of the whole number, in applications to Congress for the purpose. When new states are to be formed by a junction of two or more states, or parts of states, the legislatures of the states concerned are, as well as Congress, to concur in the measure. The states have a right also to enter into agreements or compacts, with the consent of Congress. In all such cases a communication among them results from the object which is common to them.

It is lastly to be seen, whether the confidence expressed

by the Constitution, that the *necessary and proper measures* would be taken by the other states for coöperating with Virginia in maintaining the rights reserved to the states, or to the people, be in any degree liable to the objections raised against it.

If it be liable to objections, it must be because either the object or the means are objectionable.

The object, being to maintain what the Constitution has ordained, is in itself a laudable object.

The means are expressed in the terms "the necessary and proper measures." A proper object was to be pursued by the means both necessary and proper.

To find an objection, then, it must be shown that some meaning was annexed to these general terms which was not proper; and, for this purpose, either that the means used by the General Assembly were an example of improper means, or that there were no proper means to which the terms could refer.

In the example, given by the state, of declaring the Alien and Sedition Acts to be unconstitutional, and of communicating the declaration to other states, no trace of improper means has appeared. And if the other states had concurred in making a like declaration, supported, too, by the numerous applications flowing immediately from the people, it can scarcely be doubted that these simple means would have been as sufficient as they are unexceptionable.

It is no less certain that other means might have been employed which are strictly within the limits of the Constitution. The legislatures of the states might have made a direct representation to Congress, with a view to obtain a rescinding of the two offensive acts; or they might have represented to their respective senators in Congress their wish that two thirds thereof would propose an explanatory amendment to the Constitution; or two thirds of themselves, if such had been their opinion, might, by an application to Congress, have obtained a convention for the same object.

These several means, though not equally eligible in themselves, nor probably to the states, were all constitutionally open for consideration. And if the General Assembly, after declaring the two acts to be unconstitutional, (the first and most obvious proceeding on the subject,) did not undertake to point out to the other states a choice among the further measures that might become necessary and proper, the reserve will not be misconstrued by liberal minds into any culpable imputation.

These observations appear to form a satisfactory reply to every objection which is not founded on a misconception of the terms employed in the resolutions. There is one other, however, which may be of too much importance not to be added. It cannot be forgotten that, among the arguments addressed to those who apprehended danger to liberty from the establishment of the general government over so great a country, the appeal was emphatically made to the intermediate existence of the state governments between the people and that government, to the vigilance with which they would descry the first symptoms of usurpation, and to the promptitude with which they would sound the alarm to the public. This argument was probably not without its effect; and if it was a proper one then to recommend the establishment of a constitution, it must be a proper one now to assist in its interpretation.

The only part of the two concluding resolutions that remains to be noticed, is the repetition, in the first, of that warm affection to the Union and its members, and of that scrupulous fidelity to the Constitution, which have been invariably felt by the people of this state. As the proceedings were introduced with these sentiments, they could not be more properly closed than in the same manner. Should there be any so far misled as to call in question the sincerity of these professions, whatever regret may be excited by the error, the General Assembly cannot descend into a discussion of it. Those who have listened to the suggestion can only be left to their own recollection of the part which this state has borne in the establishment of our national independence, or the establishment of our national Constitution, and in maintaining under it the authority and laws of the Union, without a single exception of internal resistance or commotion. By recurring to the facts, they will be able to convince themselves that the representatives of the people of Virginia must be above the necessity of opposing any other shield to attacks on their national patriotism, than their own conscientiousness, and the justice of an enlightened public; who will perceive in the resolutions themselves the strongest evidence of attachment both to the Constitution and the Union, since it is only by maintaining the different governments, and the departments within their respective limits, that the blessings of either can be perpetuated.

The extensive view of the subject, thus taken by the committee, has led them to report to the house, as *the result of the whole,* the following resolution:—

Resolved, That the General Assembly, having carefully

and respectfully attended to the proceedings of a number of the states, *in answer to the resolutions of December 21, 1798, and having accurately and fully reëxamined and reconsidered the latter, find it to be their indispensable duty* to adhere to the same, as founded in truth, as consonant with the Constitution, and as conducive to its preservation; and more especially to be their duty to renew, as they do hereby renew, their PROTEST against Alien and Sedition Acts, as palpable and alarming infractions of the Constitution.

Notes to the Introduction

x dealings with France "insane": "From Thomas Jefferson to James Madison, 21 March 1798," *Founders Online,* National Archives, accessed May 30, 2025, from founders.archives.gov/documents/Jefferson/01-30-02-0128. [Original source: *The Papers of Thomas Jefferson,* vol. 30, *1 January 1798–31 January 1799,* ed. Barbara B. Oberg, Princeton University Press, 2003, pp. 189–91.]

ix Indeed, leading historians: "We will misunderstand [the Founding Fathers'] politics badly if we read them so anachronistically as to imagine that they had a matured conception of a legitimate organized opposition or of a party system. . . . The Federalists and Republicans did not think of each other as alternating parties in a two-party system. Each side hoped instead to eliminate party conflict by persuading and absorbing the more acceptable and "innocent" members of the other; each side hoped to attach the stigma of foreign allegiance and disloyalty to the intractable leaders of the other, and to put them out of business as a party. The high point in Federalist efforts in this direction came with the Alien and Sedition Acts of 1798." Richard Hofstader, *The Idea of a Party System: The Rise of Legitimate Opposition in the United States, 1780–1840* (University of California Press, 1970), 8.

xii last day of Adams's term: Terri Diane Halperin, *The Alien and Sedition Acts of 1798: Testing the Constitution* (Johns Hopkins University Press, 2016), 6.

xii "a monster that must for ever disgrace his parents": "To Thomas Jefferson from James Madison, 20 May 1798," *Founders Online,* National Archives, accessed May 30, 2025, from founders.archives.gov/documents/Jefferson/01-30-02-0255. [Original source: *The Papers of Thomas Jefferson,* vol. 30, *1 January 1798–31 January 1799,* ed. Barbara B. Oberg, Princeton University Press, 2003, pp. 358–360.]

xiii But the Supreme Court has: E.g., *Chisholm v. Georgia,* 2 U.S. 419, 471 (1793).

xiii an entrenched principle in American immigration law: In 1903, more than one hundred years after the Alien Act expired, Congress provided for the deportation of aliens who were "anarchists, or persons who believe in or advocate the overthrow by force or violence of the government of the United States." 32 Stat. 1213 (1903). In 1917, this statute was expanded to allow deportation at any time rather than within three years of the alien's entry. In 1918 and 1920, Congress further expanded the scope to encompass members in any organization that "believes, teaches or advocates" the doctrines proscribed by the 1903 act—this led to scores of deportations. 40 Stat. 1012 (1918); 41 Stat. 1008 (1920). In 1940, Congress again expanded the scope to include those who were former members of such organizations. Alien Registration Act, 54 Stat. 670 (1940). In 1950 and 1952, Congress widened political bases for deportation, including past or present membership in the Communist party. Internal Security Act of 1950, 64 Stat. 987 (1950); Immigration and Nationality Act of 1952, 66 Stat. 163 (1952).

xiv the Page Act: Ch. 141, 23 Stat. 28, §§ 1–3 (1875). Repealed 1974.

xv the order described: Executive Order No. 9066 (February 19, 1942).

xv that other Asian Americans: Mary Paik Lee, *Quiet Odyssey: A Pioneer Korean Woman in America* (University of Washington Press, 1990).

xvi *Korematsu v. United States:* 323 U.S. 214 (1944).

xvi The court ruled: *Id.* at 224.

xvi he warned that: *Id.* at 202, 240.

xvi Justice Robert H. Jackson avowed: *Id.* at 248.

xvi He also highlighted: *Id.* at 245.

xvii *Ludecke v. Watkins:* 335 U.S. 160 (1948).

xvii Justice Felix Frankfurter: *Id.* at 169; *Marbury v. Madison,* 5 U.S. 137 (1803).

xvii "very great discretionary powers": *Ludecke,* 335 U.S. 164–65.

xvii "nullifies the power": *Id.* at 167.

xviii In that proclamation: *Id.* at 170; Proclamation 2714: Cessation of Hostilities (December 31, 1946).

xviii "The Founders in": *Ludecke,* 335 U.S. 171

xviii Justice Black warned: *Id.* at 174–75.

xviii "because of today's opinion": *Id.* at 183.

xviii "it is undisputed": *Id.* at 184.

xviii "The notion that": *Id.* at 187.

xx In addition to holding: *Trump v. J.G.G.,* No. 24A931, 604 U.S. __ (2025) (per curiam), slip op. at 2.

xxi the court reversed: *Id.* at 2.

xxi "the scores of": *Id.* at 16.

xxi "The implication of": *Id.* at 8.

xxii Shortly after midnight: *A.A.R.P. v. Trump,* No. 24A1007, 604 U.S. __ (Apr. 19, 2025), order at 1.

xxii Less than a month later: *A.A.R.P. v. Trump,* No. 24A1007, 605 U.S. __ (May 16, 2025) (per curiam), slip op. at 3.

xxii the court highlighted: *Id.* at 3–4.

xxii Echoing Justice Douglas's: *Id.*

xxiii President George H. W. Bush: Mintz, S., & McNeil, S. (2018). *Digital History,* accessed May 30, 2025, from digitalhistory.uh.edu/active_learning/explorations/japanese_internment/bush.cfm.

xxiv The Supreme Court has since overruled: *Trump v. Hawaii*, 585 U.S. 667, 710 (2018).

xxiv "I regret not the": "From John Adams to John Quincy Adams, 6 December 1804," *Founders Online*, National Archives, accessed May 30, 2025, from founders.archives.gov/documents/Adams/99-03-02-1354.

xxv one newspaper printer: Terri Diane Halperin, *The Alien and Sedition Acts of 1798: Testing the Constitution* (Johns Hopkins University Press, 2016), 80–84.

ABOUT THE TYPE

The principal text of this Modern Library edition was set in a digitized version of Janson, a typeface that dates from about 1690 and was cut by Nicholas Kis (1650–1702), a Hungarian working in Amsterdam. The original matrices have survived and are held by the Stempel foundry in Germany. Hermann Zapf (1918–2015) redesigned some of the weights and sizes for Stempel, basing his revisions on the original design.